CHRISTIAN UNITY

AND ITS RECOVERY.

BY

JOHN S. DAVENPORT.

NEW YORK:
D. APPLETON AND COMPANY,
443 & 445 BROADWAY.
1866.

CONTENTS.

CHAPTER IV.

THE RECOVERY OF ORGANIC UNITY.

CHAPTER V.

THEORIES OF UNITY.

CHAPTER VI.

THE ROMAN DOCTRINE OF UNITY.

CHAPTER VII.

THE CONSTITUENT UNITIES.

CHRISTIAN UNITY.

INTRODUCTION.

The divided state of Christendom is a subject that never fails to excite the deepest interest in all who truly love the Lord Jesus Christ. There is an instinct in the Christian life which forbids Christian men to rest satisfied with division. Ever since the consummation of the great schism between the East and the West, in the eleventh century, efforts have from time to time been made to heal the breach, though without any substantial success. The nearest approach to it was made by the Council of Florence, in 1439; which, however, was rendered futile by the refusal of the Greeks to assent to the reconciliation. In the next century occurred the Protestant Reformation, since when no serious efforts have been made by the Roman Church to restore the broken connection, and the principles of Protestantism preclude every wish or desire for a union with Roman Catholics.

Some members of the English Church have endeavored to fix principles of approximation on the part of that communion with the Roman Church, one consequence of which has been the secession of large numbers of her best and ablest men to Rome. But this very result has shown how utterly futile must be any attempt to reconcile these two ecclesiastical systems. Among Protestants there have been, and continue to be, discussions upon the union of various sects and churches, and a very strong feeling of the evil of division prevails.

Special interest is manifested in the subject at the present time, and it is supposed that the state of the popular religious mind is favorable to the consideration of any suggestions offered for its solution.

The interest that is felt on this subject generally, has essayed something like organization to secure the end.

1. There is, I believe, a wide-spread agreement, especially among members of the English Church, together with Episcopalians in this land, in concert with members of the Roman Catholic Church in Europe, for prayer to God to restore unity to divided Christendom. Such an agreement is always a hopeful sign of good. We know that unity is a result acceptable to God, and may be well assured that such a united prayer, going up from so many hearts, is the inspiration of the Spirit of God, who teaches the Church what to pray for. The answer may not come in the form in which many expect it, but if God's children ask for bread He will not give them a stone, and He will grant their requests in such

way that they shall know that He has heard their prayers.

2. An effort is being made on the part of the Episcopalian bodies in England and America, to bring about intercommunion between these churches and the Greek and Russo-Greek churches. When we consider the conflicting opinions on all the questions involved that prevail in these Protestant churches, to say nothing of the other party, we cannot suppose that any thing can be effected that will materially change the relations of these bodies to one another. The English Church, even if there were no other obstacles, can do nothing without the consent of the Government, and there is no probability that the Government will give assent to any movement that is at all likely to bring the Establishment into any intimate relations with other State churches; and the Episcopal Church in the United States cannot speak with any unanimity on the doctrinal and ecclesiastical questions involved. The most that can be accomplished, therefore, is the interchange of good feeling and the increase of mutual intelligence. But still, if intercommunion could be effected in the way sought for, it would come very far short of the unity which is the perfect condition of the Church.

3. The various Protestant denominations in this land, who for the most part deny any exact divine organization of the Church, are engaged in an association for Christian union, the plan of which seems to confine itself to the coöperation of the different Christian bodies,

in such good works as they can perform together without surrendering their denominational principles. This has often been tried before, but has never yet resulted in any thing practical or efficient; and in the absence of any assertion of organic principles which are to command the faith and submission of the Christian mind, it is difficult to see how any union can be effected which shall have any binding force.

In so far as these movements are indications of a conviction of the wickedness and unprofitableness of the sectarian condition of Christendom, they are worthy of respect. We may well hope that the interest which is felt in this subject is the work of the Holy Ghost, drawing the minds of men toward a true Christian unity, just as a similar tendency to organization and unity is manifested in the region of the natural.

The subject, however, needs to be discussed in the light of great principles; and the attempt has been made in the following pages, to do this from a point of view different from that commonly taken.

I. It is assumed that the unity of the Spirit is the end to be attained by the Church, and that its attainment is perfection.

II. I have then endeavored to show that the outward unity of the Church is the means of attaining the inward unity of the spirit.

III. As a preliminary to the solution of the problem of a recovered unity, I have taken a review of the present condition of Christendom with reference to unity.

IV. I have stated the method in which unity is to be recovered.

To this is added an examination of different theories of unity, and the whole is closed with some practical suggestions as to the conditions of any progress in the direction of a recovered unity.

If this effort shall have no other result than to lead some minds to a more Catholic tone of thought on this subject, it will not be in vain; and I shall hope that it may serve as a preparation for meeting future conditions of the Church, when the necessity of unity to the very existence of an organized Christianity will be manifest to all.

CHAPTER I.

THE TRUE NATURE OF UNITY CONSIDERED.

The Unity of Creation the great purpose of God in Christ—The Church to be the first example of this Unity—This the significance of Our Lord's Prayer in John, ch. xvii.—The Unity of the Father and the Son the type of Unity in the Church—What is this Unity?—What it implies in the Church—This the last and perfect attainment of the Church—The initial ground of this Unity—Its complete development—The Church originally constituted as one having lost Outward Unity has now to work back to it, that she may be prepared for the coming of her Lord.

THE great purpose of God in Christ we are told by S. Paul is, "to gather together in one head (*κεφαλαίωσασθαι*), all things in Christ, which are in heaven, and which are on earth, even in him."[1] Unity, organization, bringing all things under headship to Christ, is the work of God which extends to all creation. All beings are to have their places assigned them, and to recognize those places in subjection to the Man to whom God has given all authority and power in heaven and in Earth. The rule of Christ is to be seen and manifested in every sphere of existence, so that through Him, as the manifestation of the Invisible, God may be all in all. If this result is to be attained in all the ranks of Creation it must first of all appear in the Church, which is the company of the

[1] Ephes. i. 10.

first-born, and will, in the age to come, occupy the place of precedency over all other classes of intelligences. S. Paul writes: "Unto me, who am less than the least of all Saints, is this grace given, that I should preach among the Gentiles the unsearchable riches of Christ, and make all men see what is the fellowship of the mystery, which from the beginning of the world hath been hid in God, who created all things by Jesus Christ, to the intent that now, unto the principalities and powers in the heavenlies, may be made known by the Church, the manifold wisdom of God, according to His eternal purpose which He purposed in Christ Jesus, our Lord."[1]

The Church then—the body called out from the world in Christ—is to be the example of the fulfilment of God's purposes in Creation. It is by the Church that the divine wisdom is to be manifested, and the purpose to gather all things together in one head under Christ, is to be declared. It would follow of necessity that first of all, this unity which is the end of God's works, should be made to appear in the Church. The Church that is to witness to the creation of the heading up of all things in Christ—of the perfect organization and order of every created intelligence under the rule of the Man exalted to His Father's right hand, must, in order to such a witness, be itself constituted in unity under Him who is its head. And we can thus see the more readily what is the significance of the prayer of our Lord in the 17th chapter of John: "Neither pray I for these alone, but for them

[1] Ephes. iii. 8–10.

also that shall believe in me through their word; that they all may be one; as Thou Father art in me and I in Thee, that they also may be one in us; that the world may believe that Thou hast sent me. And the glory which Thou gavest me I have given them; that they may be one even as we are one, I in them and Thou in me, that they may be made perfect in one; and that the world may know that Thou hast sent me, and hast loved them as Thou hast loved me."[1] The Church is the organ whereby the Divine glory is to be made known, as the means of gathering into one head all things in Christ. The Divine glory is seen in the unity of the Father and the Son, and that unity can only then be manifest to the Creation, when those whom God hath chosen out of the world and given to His Son, are so united as to present an image or reflection of that unity. Hence it is, that by S. Paul the perfect result of God's actings in the Church is expressed by the attainment of unity: "Until we all come into (εις) the unity of the Faith, and of the knowledge of the Son of God, unto a perfect man, unto the measure of the stature of the fulness of Christ."[2] It is this attainment which our Lord contemplates in His intercessory prayer—the prayer which we may not doubt He continually offers for His people before His Father's throne. This prayer must have its answer, for whatever the Well-Beloved asks of the Father will surely be granted. The delay in its complete fulfilment furnishes no cause for doubting its

[1] John xvii. 20–23. [2] Ephes. iv. 13.

ultimate accomplishment. We are held to the assurance that the time will come when there shall be on earth a company of those who believe in Christ, who shall be so united one to another, as to realize this unity here described—the unity which subsists between the Father and the Son.

This now is the unity of the Spirit, which S. Paul exhorts the Ephesian Christians to preserve—"endeavoring to keep the unity of the Spirit in the bond of peace." [1] It had its exemplification at the beginning of the Gospel dispensation. It existed and was a thing to be zealously kept. There were causes even then in operation, as we learn from the Epistles to the Corinthians, the Philippians, the Galatians, the Hebrews, and indeed from almost all the Epistles, which threatened to disturb it; these causes have for centuries operated to such an extent in Christendom, that the problem now is, not how to preserve unity, but how to recover it.

The unity thus referred to is something deeper and more mysterious than any mere ecclesiastical unity, however necessary that may be for its attainment. It is something more real and vital than any consent or agreement of sects one with another. It is a unity which has no parallel in human or finite relations: "That they may be one; as Thou Father art in me and I in Thee, that they also may be one in us (I in them and Thou in me), that they may be made perfect in one." It is a unity that results from believers partaking of the

[1] Ephes. iv. 3.

glory which the Father gave to the Son, and which He had given to them. The more we attempt to comprehend this mystery, the more does it appear to pass all understanding. What can we say of that unity, which is thus set forth as the type of the spiritual unity in the Church? What is the unity of the Father and the Son? On such a topic we must speak and write very reverently, lest we should be intruding into what is not revealed. But as this is set before us as the type of the unity of the Church, we may venture to look into it with such light as Holy Scripture casts upon it.

The unity of the Father and the Son consists in the participation by each of the Divine Persons of the same substance, and their possession of one and the same Spirit (who is also a Person), while yet their personality is unimpaired, and while there is a different sphere of actings of the two Divine persons; still there is that relation between them that the acts of each become the acts of the other. The Father is the source of all Being. The Son is begotten of the Father, and it is by Him that the will of the Father is carried out. The Spirit proceedeth from the Father, and is the giver of life to all creation; but the Spirit which proceedeth from the Father is also in the Son, and proceedeth from the Son, and herein is the bond of unity. In every man there is one individual spirit which is in him and not in another. No man can impart his own life to another, or cause his spirit to reside in another. Hence, though all men are partakers of the same nature, and in this respect are one, yet is not the unity complete. In the Father and the Son, however, there is one Spirit who is also a Person and who can reside in both, so that here is a unity not conceivable among creatures. The Son is in the Father, and the Father is in the Son.

As this therefore is the unity of the Divine persons, so does the unity of the members of the Body of Christ consist in this, that as they are by the Holy Ghost partakers of the one nature of Christ, and thus He is "in them," so they are by virtue of their union to Him one with the Father also—"I in them and Thou in me"—and therefore in the highest sense one with another. There is among the members of Christ a mystical union, to Him and to one another, which lies quite out of the region of natural modes of conception, and is known only by Faith. This is clearly implied in such passages of Scripture as the following: "Abide in me and I in you. As the branch cannnot bear fruit of itself except it abide in the vine, no more can ye except ye abide in me. I am the vine, ye are the branches. He that abideth in me and I in him, the same bringeth forth much fruit; for without me ye can do nothing. If a man abide not in me, he is cast forth as a branch and is withered, and men gather them and cast them into the fire, and they are burned. If ye abide in me and I in you, ye shall ask what ye will and it shall be done unto you."[1] "Know ye not that so many of us as were baptized into Jesus Christ were baptized into His death? Therefore we are

[1] John xv. 4–8.

buried with Him by Baptism into death, that like as Christ was raised from the dead by the glory of the Father, even so we also should walk in newness of life," &c.[1] "And now little children abide in Him, that when He shall appear ye may have confidence and not be ashamed before Him at His coming."[2] What is implied in these words is an actual relation to Christ, which is not mere verbal, or external, but real and vital, as proceeding from the participation of His life; and as all who truly believe in Christ and conform to His commandments are said to be in Him—to be members of Christ—members of His body, of His flesh, and of His bones, so must they also be one with each other.

The unity of the Father and the Son involves also the most perfect oneness of mind and purpose. There are no varying purposes, no divergent actions of the Divine persons. "The Son can do nothing of Himself, but what He seeth the Father do; for what things soever the Father doeth those also doeth the Son likewise." "I came not to do mine own will, but the will of the Father which sent me." And to complete the parallel, there must be among the members of Christ the same identity of will, of purpose, and of affection—all in subordination to the Head.

Such a perfect unity as is shadowed forth in the prayer of our Lord is the last and perfect attainment of the Church. It is a result to be arrived at, not one which is perfect from the beginning. This is apparent

[1] Rom. vi. 3, 4, &c. [2] John ii. 28.

from the words of St. Paul already referred to: "Till we all come into the unity of the faith and of the knowledge of the Son of God unto a perfect man, to the measure of the stature of the fulness of Christ." Here attainment is contemplated, growth, which shall result in perfect unity. This is involved in the words, too, of the intercessory prayer. The Lord asked his Father, not only that His disciples might partake of that grace which should unite them into one body, but that the unity of the body might be preserved and developed, until there should be found in the body of the faithful, a oneness which should be parallel with that of the Father and the Son. The prayer looks to an end. Nothing is implied in its terms as to the time when that end shall be reached. It contemplates a working in a body, which can only be complete as that body attains its maturity. When that end is attained, then the Bride will be perfect and prepared for the marriage, and the Bridegroom will come and take her to Himself. The time, therefore, that is covered by this prayer is the entire period of the Christian dispensation, during which the Church is being perfected. It is a result not yet attained, but which must be in a process of attainment.

The unity of the Spirit, therefore, may be considered under the two heads of its initial ground and its complete development.

I. From the Holy Scriptures we learn that it is by the ordinance of baptism that men are initiated into a participation in the unity of the Body. "By one Spirit are we all baptized into one body, whether we be Jew or Gentile, whether we be bond or free;"[1] "As many of you as were baptized unto Jesus Christ were baptized into His death;" and thus by baptism are "planted together," both in the likeness of His death and of His resurrection.[2] For this reason it is proper to say that all the baptized, speaking generally, have a participation in the unity of the Body; they are, in some sense, members of the body of Christ. This is what we call the "initial ground" of unity. It is based upon the incarnation of the Word. The Son of God came into our nature and became completely one with humanity, a member of the race, of which He was constituted the new head. Taking our nature into union with His own, He cleansed and purified it. Passing through the grave and gate of death, He destroyed in it all remains of corruption and infirmity; and rising from the dead and ascending to the Father, He presented our nature in His resurrection body to His Father, pure and undefiled. Through the operation of the Holy Ghost He imparts to those who believe in Him the virtue of His resurrection life, by partaking of which they dwell in Him and He in them. This participation is not a mere influence, it is not a mere moral effect produced in the region of the mind and affections. It is an actual imparting of the vital energy of His own resurrection body, which thus becomes a new life. It is the introduction of a new vital element, which renders possible a true spiritual obedience. The

[1] 1 Cor. xii. 13.

[2] Rom. vi. 4, 5.

introduction of this supernatural principle, then, is the element of unity. It is not natural life which is the basis of unity, but a supernatural life, which, by the operation of the Holy Ghost, comes from the person of the Incarnate Word, risen from the dead and entered into a spiritual body.

If the inquiry should arise, How is this possible—the transmission of the life of Jesus to men? the answer is twofold:

First. The same which the Lord gave to the Capernaites when they said, "How can this man give us his flesh to eat?" "What if ye shall see the Son of Man ascend up where He was before? It is the Spirit that quickeneth, the flesh profiteth nothing." The change from the natural to the spiritual body, and its ascension to heaven, alters the case. This man, as you now see Him, cannot give you His flesh to eat—can do nothing answering to that form of words; but in the spiritual body He may impart it to you as a spiritual substance. What is absurd in one state of facts is admissible in another. And so the conditions which are applicable to the natural life of a man, do not hold with reference to the spiritual nature of Him who is the Word made flesh. We cannot argue from the case of the natural to the supernatural. It is a matter of faith. All that can be said by way of argument upon the subject, is to show that there is no presumption against it.

Secondly. One human spirit cannot impart its own substance to another; but this limitation does not apply to the Divine Spirit. The mystery of the Trinity extends itself to the body of Christ. As the one Spirit is in the Father and the Son, so does He, proceeding from both the Father and the Son, also impart the life of the Son, incarnate and glorified, to the members of the Church. The Church is the temple of the Holy Ghost, and He dwells personally in every member of the Church in whom the conditions of a perfect unity with Christ are fulfilled. The faith which admits the Trinity, need find no difficulty in the truth of the oneness of the baptized with Christ.

It is thus that in the initiatory sacrament, there is implanted in the spiritual constitution of the baptized the germ of that spiritual life, which, in its perfect maturity, develops into perfect unity.

We come, therefore, to consider the second head under which the unity of the spirit is to be considered.

II. The element or germ of unity being thus implanted by the impartation of a supernatural life, remains to be developed to its manifestation, in the collective body of those who believe in Christ through His Word, ministered in His Church. This result involves an entire unity of faith, of hope, of purpose, of affection; and where this exists, there will be the perfect unity of the Spirit—the Lord's prayer will have been answered.

First of all to be attained is "unity of faith and of the knowledge of the Son of God." Without this, all apparent unity is delusive. It has been the instinct of the divine life in the Church resisting separation, which has in past ages maintained the conflict for the integrity and unity of Christian doctrine. There has ever been a deep conviction of the necessity of an entire agreement in all that was properly *de fide*—all that related to the knowledge of God and of Jesus Christ. However much controversy may have been embittered by personal interests and worldly motives, yet the teachers and confessors of past ages—those who, like Athanasius, have withstood a world in defence of the last iota of truth—have been impelled by the conviction, that the very existence of the Church depended on the maintenance, unimpared, of the faith once delivered to the saints. The heretics have in all ages been ready to assent to a variety of creeds—a difference in forms of expression for declaring the most fundamental and eternal truths—those in which Christianity as a system consists; while the party that has contended for the unity of the body has always been strenuous for the assertion of fixed forms of faith.

It is manifest that differing dogmas will and must result in differing sentiments and practical conclusions. The office of the Gospel, fully administered, is to "cast down imaginations and every high thing that exalteth itself against the knowledge of God, and to bring every thought in subjection to the obedience of Christ." The truth is one thing and not another. There may be some things relating to the religious life which are matters of opinion; but this is not the case with those which relate to the knowledge of the Son of God. Two differing opinions cannot be equally admissible concerning the person or the work of Christ, or His relation to His followers or to the Church. One or the other must be wrong, and it belongs to the Church, as the witness for the truth, to define doctrine and say, "This is the Catholic faith, which except a man believe faithfully he cannot be saved."[1] It is the part of faith to submit to divine revelation—and opinion is not faith. There is no faith where one is doubtful whether what he believes is or is not the very truth of God. The admission of a variety of beliefs in the Church would unsettle every belief, so that no faith were possible.

St. Paul is very urgent upon the Churches to maintain perfect unity of conviction. To the Corinthians he writes (1 Cor. i. 10): "Now I beseech you, brethren, by the name of our Lord Jesus Christ, that ye all speak the same thing, and that there be no divisions among you, but that ye be perfectly joined together in the same mind and in the same judgment." To the Philippians (ch. iii. 3): "If there be, therefore, any consolation in Christ, if any fellowship of the Spirit, if any bowels and mercies, fulfil ye my joy that ye be like-minded, having the same love, being of one accord, of one mind." To the Thessalonians (2d Epis. ii. 15): "Therefore stand fast and hold the traditions which ye have been taught, whether by word or our epistle." These and other passages, having a similar bearing, make it apparent that a complete and unbroken unity in the intellectual conviction of every member of the body, in respect to all that

[1] Athanasian creed.

can be called the knowledge of Christ—all that relates to Him in every aspect of His work—is the most essential condition or prerequisite of the unity of spirit which is implied in our Lord's prayer. To specify doctrines would give a direction to this discussion which is not intended, and is therefore avoided; but we may say this, that in order to the realization of unity, there must be such an exhaustive and comprehensive method of recognized teaching on the matters of faith, as shall preclude all controversy, and shall cover every question which can possibly arise as a cause of separation. The Church, the body of the faithful, must reach such an attainment. The idiosyncrasies of intellect which strive to assert themselves must be mastered by the truth. The peculiarities of disposition, of temperament, of natural life, even, must give way so far as to recognize what truly comes from God. The pride of life, the consciousness of power and of intelligence, which arrays itself against the authority of the Lord, must be sacrificed. Spiritual truths are manifested in opposite (not opposing) poles, and much of the division which has given rise to sects, has resulted from parties considering one side of the truth, to the exclusion of the other. Of this the Calvinistic and Arminian controversies of our own time furnish a pertinent example. There is truth in both sides, and it is the office of a true spiritual discernment to see both sides of the truth in harmony. The intellectual tendencies of different classes of persons have led them to assert the one and the other side as the exclusive truth, while the mind that is regulated not by its own natural tendencies, but by the faith which is the gift of God, will embrace the truth contained in both sides, and contemplate them in harmony as one. Such a reconciliation is not of the nature of compromise—does not involve the surrender of a truth or the admission to an equal standing with it of an error, but it is the victory of faith over the divisive tendencies of the fleshly intellect. Faith wrought by the Holy Ghost is operative in the spirit and works by love. It is light in the intellect, and life and energy in the will. Faith is unity so far as it is spiritual and not corrupted by the fleshly understanding. The things in which faithful men differ, are either matters of opinion which are not faith, or points which have little or no relation to their belief, and should never be brought into religious controversy.

The attainment of this unity of Faith and of the knowledge of the Son of God, is the complete development of the Spiritual life imparted to the baptized. It is the result of growth, not the effect of argument or controversy. It is effected by the Holy Ghost working in the body of the baptized, and knitting them together into one. When realized, it will be the answer to the prayer of the Lord, that they all may be one, for then the one Spirit which is in the Father and the Son, abiding also in the Church, will effect unity of knowledge, unity of purpose, unity of love. The will of the Father will be the controlling will of the whole body. The knowledge of the Son, as the manifestation of the Father, will be the light lighting every man. The carrying out of the purpose of God as manifested in His Son will be the sole desire and intent of every individual member; while the perfect love which casteth out fear, the love of God shed abroad in the heart, and extending itself to all creation, will be the perfection of the chain of unity.

The Church was born in the unity of the Spirit, so that St. Paul when he wrote could say without the need of any qualification, "There is one body." There had as yet arisen no schism in the body. There were not two or more companies of Christians claiming each to be the Church or fragments of the Church. No outward breach of unity of the Spirit had occurred, and so the exhortation was to *preserve* what already existed.

But the Faith out of which this unity sprang was as yet immature. It needed to be tried, and in the trial its integrity yielded. The spirit of schism early entered and continued to work. St. Paul himself foretold an apostacy, and one of its results is the schism of which we now see the fruits. The unity of the Spirit does not prevail, and believers are not one as the Father and the Son are one. There can be no unity of Spirit when sects are allowed or recognized.

The Church now, therefore, has to work back to the unity which once she possessed and has lost. Her great work is to recover the unity of the Spirit, so that it can again be said in fact as well as in idea, "there is one body." She has to "grow up in all things into Him who is the head, even Christ," so that there may be found on

2

earth a body, which has attained to the knowledge of the Son of God in its perfection. She has to outgrow or throw off every thing that belongs not to the very essence of the Faith. She has to enlarge her understanding of the Gospel, so as to recognize and embrace every thing that does belong to, or legitimately flow from the true doctrine of Christ as revealed in God's word. The work of recovering unity involves not contraction but enlargement. It is not elimination, but expansion, that is required. Not breadth, but narrowness, is the cause of schism. It is not affirmation but negation which has given origin to sects. The Church is built doctrinally upon the affirmation of the truth of the Incarnation. It is the refusal to affirm and recognize this truth in all its bearings that has been the occasion of schism. Negation limits the view and restricts the flow of charity. Perfect unity takes in every fragment of truth and every form of its practical realization, whether in doctrine, in organization, in worship, or in morals, and assigns to every truth its place in the entire system. This statement might be illustrated by particulars, but for the wish to avoid a polemical tone in this discussion; but it is historically true. Every truly Christian sentiment has its origin in the Catholic faith, and that faith therefore must be sufficient to comprehend them all.

Such a unity of Spirit must be attained before the Church can be prepared to be received by her Lord, "as a bride adorned for her husband." "My dove, my undefiled is one." Whether this unity shall include all the baptized or not, it is certain that there must be a company on the earth, in whom the unity of the Father and the Son shall have its manifestation, so that it shall be a witness to the world. It would be according to analogies in nature and in grace, that such a recovered unity should spring from a nucleus, gathering to itself those who might be found prepared to receive the truth, so that they might "grow up into Him who is the head in all things," expanding until the full number necessary to its perfection should be gathered in. The effecting of such a unity is the crowning work of the Holy Ghost in the Church. It is the last and highest result and application of the life of Jesus in this present dispensation. Only one thing more remains to fulfil the work of salvation, and that is the raising of the dead in Christ. This will not be done until the Lord Himself comes forth from His Father's right hand, and a new series of divine acts begins. Perfect unity is the highest manifestation of the power which is now dispensed by Him through the Holy Ghost from His Father's right hand. This power is competent to overcome every hindrance, and bring about a complete and perfect accordance in all things in the Body of Christ.

CHAPTER II.

ORGANIC UNITY THE MEANS OF SECURING THE UNITY OF THE SPIRIT.

No Unity of Spirit where there are Sects—Unity of Spirit not to be attained without Means—Are there any Divine Ordinances for the Preservation of Unity found in the Constitution of the Ministry?—What is meant by Organic Unity?—The True Constitution of the Church impressed upon her by the Lord—The Divine Constitution of the Church the means of bringing into Subjection, 1, the Will; 2, the Intellect; 3, the Affections—Universality necessary to its Effect

WE have hitherto been regarding the unity of the Spirit, in which consists the perfect attainment of the Church. Unity is an end, not only a means. We are to desire unity, not merely for the strength it will give against enemies, or for the sake of increasing the number of conversions, but because the Church is the sphere, where first of all, the great purpose of God to gather all things under one head in Christ is to be exemplified. The attainment of this unity is the very chiefest result of the probation of the Church. In the Church first, is this perfect subordination to a head, and perfect union in the head to be seen, that the world at large may also receive the manifestation of the Father through the Son.

It is too manifest to need sober argument, that unity

of spirit cannot exist where there are sects. Sects arise from an imperfect faith—an imperfect knowledge of the Son of God. They involve differing views of matters relating to the faith. They imply the absence of any bond of peace whereby to preserve unity. Where there are sects, men are not "perfectly joined together in the same mind and in the same judgment" (1 Cor. i. 10). Sects arise from "one saying I am of Paul, and I of Apollos, and I of Cephas" (1 Cor. i. 12). Sects spring either from difference of doctrine concerning Christ Himself and His way of salvation, or from differing views of the relation He sustains to His Church and the way in which it should be ruled, or from preferences as to worship, or worst of all, from some merely sectional, national, or personal interests. How absurd, then, to talk of unity of spirit in the midst of sects! The fact most sorrowful of all in this day, next to the existence of sects, is, that many are found who defend sectarianism on principle, as a condition of the Church acceptable to God and profitable to men. No union of sects where such principles are maintained, is any approach to unity. The very first element of unity is wanting.

The unity of the Spirit cannot be attained without means. The work of the Holy Ghost is not immediately upon men, but mediately, through ordinances. For every appointed result in the Church, there is a means appointed by God. For the attainment of every end there is an ordinance, and we cannot suppose that an end so near the heart of our dear Lord as this one of unity, should not be provided for specially, in the system of means and ordinances which He left for the perfecting of His Church. For let it be remembered that although there is in the Church even in its state of separation, an instinctive desire and longing for unity, yet the instinct is not so powerful as to make sure of its own aim, or such that unity can be realized without severe spiritual effort. Moreover, it is effected by the operation of the Holy Ghost, and, according to all the analogies of divine working, this special operation requires ordinances adapted to the result.

Have we in Holy Scripture any intimation of any system of ordinances appointed for this purpose? Nothing can be more clear than the words of St. Paul, in Ephes. iv. 1–13. Here he urges the obligation to "walk worthy of the vocation wherewith we are called." That is, we are called as members of one body, in which is to be made manifest the purpose of God to gather all things together into one head under Christ. This "worthiness" consists in the exercise of lowliness, meekness, long suffering and forbearance, as the correctives of that pride and self-seeking which are the provocatives of schism. In all this it is easy to see, the apostle anticipates and aims to guard against the very sins and infirmities which have in fact been the originating causes of the existing schisms. What but pride, and jealousy, and self-will, originated the great schism of the East and the West, and all subsequent schisms of which we now see the fruits? Then, after stating the absolute grounds of unity, in the essential oneness of body, in the fact of the body being dwelt in and inspired by one Spirit, and animated by one hope in the one Lord, one faith, one baptism, one God and Father of all, he proceeds to declare what was the divine ordinance given for the preservation of unity. "Wherefore He saith, when He ascended up on high, He led captivity captive, and gave gifts unto men; and He gave some [men] apostles, and some prophets, and some evangelists, and some pastors and teachers, for the perfecting of the saints to the work of ministry, for the edifying of the body of Christ, until we all come into the unity of the faith, and of the knowledge of the Son of God, unto a perfect man, unto the measure of the stature of the fulness of Christ." Now, from this it is very clear that the divine constitution of the ministry is the ordinance for the preservation and perfection of unity; and as the constitution of the ministry involves the constitution of the Church, we are justified in drawing the inference that *outward organic unity is the divinely ordained means of attaining the perfect unity of the Spirit.*

By organic unity is meant *the unity of the whole Church throughout the world in one organization.*

The means precedes the end, as the end presupposes and implies the means. The Church is the mother of us all. The organization is before those who are added to it. The Lord added to the Church daily those who were saved (σωζομενους, Acts ii. 47). The Lord first constituted His Church in the twelve, and sent her forth into the world to bear a witness for His name, and when that witness was effectual, those who received it were "added to the Church." Their receiving the witness and believing the word did not make them members of the Church. It was necessary that they should be baptized in the name of the Lord Jesus, and by this act they became members; and being members in that one body, were bound to preserve the unity of the body by avoiding every thing that tended to division. Now, what was it first of all that tended to preserve unity? Manifestly it was the authority of the Lord in His Apostles. "They continued steadfastly in the Apostles' doctrine and fellowship, and breaking of bread"—or, communion—"and prayers." Here the Apostles, acting collectively, were the bond of unity to the whole flock. They were the depositories of the authority of Christ the Lord. This authority, recognized in those who were sent by the Lord, bound men together. The Church was not formed and kept together merely by voluntary consent. Its bond was, subjection to authority. St. Paul declared that he was "under the law to Christ." The Church was the centre of spiritual liberty, but it was not a liberty unrestrained by law. Jesus is the Man to whom the Father hath given all authority and power. That authority He has placed in His Church, which stands as His representative on earth, and, as a spiritual mother, is charged with authority over her children. The divinely appointed organ by which that authority shall be primarily and ultimately exercised, is the apostolic office.

It is not for the Church to attempt to frame her own constitution for herself—to appoint the organs by which this or that function shall be exercised—to modify or adapt her constitution to the changes of the times. This would be to make the Church not the creation of God, but the contrivance of man. The very name of the *body of Christ* would seem enough to contradict any such conceit. The Church is left in the world as a witness for God, and we know that all that is in the world, or that belongs to it, is enmity against God. Therefore the Church can take nothing from the world. Her office is to mould society, not to be moulded by it. It is to present the ideal of perfection drawn from the divine word, not to assume the ideas which society may propose.

Nothing can be clearer than that the Lord impressed upon the Church the form that He intended it should receive. "God hath set some in the Church, first Apostles, secondarily prophets, thirdly teachers," &c. "God hath set the members, every one of them, in the body as it hath pleased Him." "God hath tempered the body together, having given more abundant honor to that part which lacked, that there may be no schism—or division—in the body."[1] How, with such words of Holy Scripture in view, any one can assert a right on the part of the collective membership of the Church to modify its constitution, is amazing; the very analogy too of *one body*, is against any such assumption. It is a body, and not a

[1] 1 Cor. xii. 18, 24, 28.

mere aggregation of individuals. No society called a body existing by law, or in any other way than as a mere voluntary association, can change or modify its organic law. That can only be done by the power that gave it being. The attempt to change the organization of the natural body, can result only in death or deformity.

Now it is this organization, thus divinely formed, which is the ordained means of effecting and bringing to perfection that unity of the Spirit which is the great object of desire in the Lord's intercessory prayer. It is ordained for this purpose, and is adapted to the end. The perfection of unity, as we have seen, involves the bringing of every thought into subjection to the obedience of Christ. The will—the understanding—the affections, all must be made to perfectly coincide with the will of God, in order that the Holy Ghost may work effectually in the members of the Body of Christ, to produce that unity which is answerable to the unity of the Father and the Son; and it is by the external unity of the Church that this effect is produced.

1. The unity of the Church is the means for the probation of man's will.

It is by authority, manifesting the will of the superior, that the will of man is brought into subjection. God has provided for this in the series of subordinations which are established in society. The relation of parent and child meets us at our entrance into life. The first waking consciousness recognizes the will of a superior by which the child is to be controlled, and in this is laid the foundation of all organized social life. Obedience to parents is the very essence of filial piety, and in the earlier years before the powers of discernment are developed, the spirit of filial obedience is doubtless an atonement for many acts in themselves evil which are performed under its promptings. The moral judgment may indeed be fearfully perverted in such cases, but there is a compensation in the control which is acquired over the will, and in a will early made subject to a lawful authority lies the secret of many a case of recovery from an almost hopeless degradation. If we were compelled to make a choice between a will duly subjected under a perverted moral training, and a high culture of the moral sentiments in which the spirit of obedience was wanting, it is hardly to be doubted that the former would be chosen. It is an anomaly, indeed, to speak of high moral culture where the will is not brought into subjection to authority; but we know that it is a fact of frequent occurrence, that families in which there is the nicest sense of honor, the highest disposition to recognize the rights of others, and the most refined sensibility to every thing that is beautiful, grow up without any adequate idea of subjection to authority. Under the mistaken notion that every thing must be carried by love, no restraint is ever placed upon the wills of children; and while great sensibility of nature may act as a preservative against vice and immorality, yet there is wanting that central element of a well-formed character—a will subdued to the recognition of law. The publicans and the harlots, with their perverted social morality, go into the kingdom of heaven before the puritanic Pharisee with his self-will in the ascendant.

To the child, while he is a child, the parent stands in God's stead. As intelligence expands, and the perception of God's commandments gains place in the mind, the respect for parental authority will of necessity undergo modification, as it is discovered whether that authority is in conformity with, or opposed to God's commandments. And here oftentimes there will arise questions of personal duty, and strugglings with doubt and difficulty, which will require prayer and spiritual counsel to determine. But there is a long period before this, during which no question can arise in the mind of a child but that of obedience, and it is then that the will is to be brought into subjection to the divine authority residing in the parent.

As we advance to the age of citizenship we are brought under the control of the authority of the State, which is another of the forms in which the authority of God is brought down to men, and the will of man is kept in subjection. This is another of the great moral agencies which God has established to prepare men in the natural sphere for that which must be perfected in the spiritual. "That is not first which is spiritual, but that which is natural, and afterwards that which is spiritual." These arrangements in the natural order for subduing the wills of men all look to the great end of God to bring every thing in subjection to His Son; and their consideration prepares us to recognize a corresponding arrangement in the spiritual order, to perfect the subjection of man's will to God.

The Church is the repository of a divine authority. As members of the Church, we are not subject to any other authority than what is involved in that relation. We all stand there individually responsible to the Lord for our acts as members of the body. After childhood, the parent's rule does not enter here, however much influence may and should prevail, and the intrusion of the rule of the State is usurpation. It is a relation in which there is the most complete exercise of personal responsibility. That self-will, disturbing the fixed order of things, is as liable to assert itself here as anywhere else, and even more so, since there are no material restraints upon it, is obvious from all history. And how is it to be restrained, and the will of man to be led to a true spiritual obedience, but by the recognition of a true divine authority in the body? If the Church is a mere voluntary association, with a constitution framed by its members and subject to their amendment, what is there to bring the will of man into subjection? Men cannot reverence what they themselves create. For the sake of policy, they may conform to rules which they have had a hand in framing; but in such a case there is wanting any influence whatever to act upon that element of their moral and spiritual nature which has the most to do with the spiritual character.

To effect this result of subduing the will, the constitution of the Church must be at once definite, divine, and unalterable except by divine revelation. There must be a line which no self-willed action can pass—a fixed order to which every will must conform. Without this, discipline can have no salutary spiritual effect, and it will be well if the exercise of self-will does not extend itself, to the choice of what parts of the divine word shall be obeyed or disregarded.

Breaches of unity arising from this as well as from every other source, are most likely to spring from the spirit of rebellion or self-will on the part of teachers, or persons holding prominent situations in the Church, and of course it is upon them that the bearing of any ordinance for the support of unity will be first felt; but they could not effect schism without a following, and the same force of authority needs to be recognized by private members as well, in order that the effect of keeping the will in subjection to the obedience of Christ may be secured. The idea of the unity of the body, and the necessity of preserving it, of the sinfulness of schism, is that which, if duly apprehended, will restrain any teacher or ruler in the body from setting up his own will against existing authority, and will be a guard to all private members against readily following the lead of those who cause divisions and contentions. It has indeed been often the case during the history of the Church in the ages, that ecclesiastical power has been wickedly used for the destruction of those who have asserted only the truth as it is in Jesus: and such things may occur again—nay are occurring at this very day before our eyes; but the part of a faithful Christian in such cases is, to put the ecclesiastical power in the wrong by leaving to it the initiative in the work of separation. That makes the power the schismatic before God, and He will judge it in His own way. To go about to overthrow any ecclesiastical authority lawfully existing, cannot be justifiable, even though that authority as actually exercised contains within itself many elements of evil. Such an effort counteracts the very purpose of God in the unity of the Church—the subjection of man's will to authority. Even an illegitimate authority exercised in the name of the Church should not be readily assailed, for it is better for Christian people to be held in control by an authority which has for them a divine sanction, than not to recognize any authority at all.

The great spiritual result of bringing the whole man into subjection to the obedience of Christ, requires an objective organization, recognized as divine and unchangeable, acting upon the will and restraining every effort at separation. In the absence of any material instruments to enforce its authority it is truly spiritual, and its action is entirely consistent with spiritual freedom, while yet as the embodiment of an idea or principle of divine revelation, as a divine ordinance, its control over the conscience is complete and adequate to the end proposed.

2. The objective unity of the Church is a discipline for man's intellect.

The Gospel is represented as "casting down imaginations, or reasonings (λογισμούς), and every high thing that exalteth itself against the knowlege of God." In these words, doubtless, reference is had to the intellectual hindrances and obstructions to a perfect obedience. Every one knows that there has been no such fruitful cause of schism in the Church as the exercise of intellectual subtilty. This, even more than resistance to authority, has broken the bond of peace whereby the unity of the Spirit was to be preserved. All the controversies of the earlier centuries were the result of attempts by the subtle oriental intellect, either to explain or develop in their own way the mysteries of the faith, or to remove the difficulties which divine revelation presented to the finite understanding. Arianism with its modern progeny of Unitarianism, Universalism, and Pantheism is the fruit of the refusal of the human intellect to submit itself to divine revelation, and of its determination to judge the word of God by its own narrow lights. The doctrine of transubstantiation is the fruit of scholastic subtilty, attempting to define a spiritual mystery in the forms of human speech.

The very culture and elevation which Christianity brings with it, excites the intellectual faculties to that degree of activity that they would fain exercise themselves on the very problems that revelation discloses. All the questions that exercised the genius of Plato and Aristotle, here present themselves, enlarged and extended by the new relations into which men are brought by the incarnation. "By faith we understand that the ages were constituted by the word of God." Here is a first truth, in receiving which the Christian philosopher is far in advance of Aristotle. Here is the certain knowledge of a personal deity—the Maker and Source of all things. But this being admitted, it is easy to bring faith to an arrest, and attempt to bring every farther truth suggested under the survey of the intellect. God is personal—but the words of Holy Scripture lead also to a Trinity. How does this Trinity exist? Is this a Trinity of persons, or only a Trinity of faculties, or of modes of manifestation? What constitutes the Trinity, and what are the relations of the members of it to one another? God has manifested himself in human form. From this flow questions of the nature of the incarnation—whether the Son of God who appeared in man's nature was really a divine person of the same substance with His Father, or a creature—whether the nature He took was really united with the divine, or a mere form which He laid aside after His Resurrection—and so on, for we do not propose to give a catalogue of heresies.

The very subjects of revelation, therefore, are those which more than any others excite intellectual activity, and this fact creates the necessity for some agency, which shall hold the self-asserting intellect in check. The Christian is not perfect until his intellect as well as his will is entirely subject to God and to His Christ. He must be content to know every thing by faith—by communication from God through His revealed word. He must be willing that even the natural reason which God has given him, and which in the natural sphere is the true organ of knowing, should stand aside and take its light and its direction from the word of God. Every reasoning (λογισμος), every high theory or philosophy, which exalteth itself against the knowledge of God, must be cast down and made subject to God's word as revealed through his Son. If theories cannot be made to harmonize with revelation, theories must give way. Until this is done in the body, the unity of the spirit cannot be perfect; we do not come into the unity of the faith and of the knowledge of the Son of God.

Now for the attainment of this result the objective unity of the Church is the only adequate means.

The Holy Scriptures are not written in a dogmatic form. Their structure seems designed to test the faith and docility of those to whom they are given. That by themselves they cannot determine doctrine, is manifest from the fact that they are appealed to by every sect that professes to be Christian at all. This is no reason for withholding them from universal perusal however, since the Church duly constituted is equal to the counteraction of false teachings, and beyond this there must be room for the exercise of individual responsibility in their use. Different interpretations are the work of different self-asserting minds, which have force enough to draw disciples after them. The only corrective of such eccentricities is the sense of obligation to preserve the unity of the Spirit. The Church received from the Apostles the form of doctrine into which all her teachings were to be cast. Every teacher is bound to teach in accordance with the analogy of the faith, and to interpret Holy Scripture in harmony with the general sense of Christendom. No one acting upon such a principle, and deeply impressed with the sin of causing a schism in the body, would ever have originated novel intepretations, much less have attempted to impose them as additions to the faith. Had Arius recognized the importance of preserving unity, he never would have outraged the convictions of the greater part of the Church by the avowal of his philosophy. Take the case of the separation of the East and West—the pretext for which was the doctrine of the double Procession. Whatever might be true, and however the Western Church might have received it, a proper regard for unity would have restrained the Roman Patriarch from attempting to enforce this faith upon the whole Church, beyond what the East had acknowledged in her creed. In the unfolding of Christian doctrine there must of necessity be a difference in the progressive development of different minds and different regions; and the only test that can be applied in such cases, is the integrity of the faith which is common to the whole Church.

The true effect of a regard for unity would be, on the part of teachers, to restrain the ambition and self-conceit which leads them to put forth new theories, and on the part of the taught, to lead them to weigh well the teachings which may result in such a disaster as a schism. Such self-restraint does not of necessity involve any intellectual bondage. It only tends to promote carefulness in the unfolding of what may be regarded by the teacher as a more advanced view of truths which the Church approves, and a willingness to subject one's self to the oversight and correction of whatever authority there may be for pronouncing upon such questions. To such supervision and review no one who knows his own insufficiency will object.*

The truth of the Gospel has a germinative power. Its province is to grow, its nature is to develop. The well-instructed scribe brings out of his treasure, things new as well as old; but the new must not be at variance with the old. Growth is essential to the attainment of unity, "that we be no more children tossed to and fro, and carried about with every wind of doctrine, but speaking the truth in love, may grow up in all things unto Him who is the head, even Christ" (Ephes. iv. 14, 15). But it is manifest that all intellectual activity is not a sign of spiritual growth. The time was foretold when "men would not endure sound doctrine, but according to their own lusts should heap to themselves teachers having itching ears; and they shall turn away their ears from the truth, and shall be turned unto fables"

* I am treating the question here in the abstract, and upon the hypothesis that the Church is perfectly constituted according to the divine will. I do not mean to deny that the state of Christendom has been such as to make it necessary for men to speak against what has been the current opinions of the time. But even reformers, in raising their voice against prevalent corruptions and perversions of doctrine, have always appealed to the general sense of Christendom in its purer days, in justification of interpretations which the Church of their own day condemned them for.

(2 Tim. iv. 3, 4). Any exercise of the intellect on spiritual subjects which is not in the direction of faith, is not spiritual progress, but a hindrance rather. Now, what is there so well calculated to restrain such an exercise of the fleshly intellect, as a conviction of the duty of avoiding any thing that may disturb the unity of the Church?

As a matter of fact, the doctrine that has obtained the universal assent of Christendom, is that which was declared by the entire Church while the whole Church was in a condition to utter her voice in ecumenical councils. Other questions have since arisen, which, for the want of any means of obtaining the universal expression of Christendom, still remain open. Schisms from schisms have resulted, of which the most obvious effect is to illustrate the necessity of a deeper conviction of the obligation of unity. The spirit of unity may exist even in the midst of schism, and it will be found wherever there is a conviction that any further division is to be avoided. Members of a sect may be so impressed with the duty of maintaining unity, as to be led thereby to restrain themselves from any indulgence of self-will that would renew division. How much more powerful must this conviction prove when it is felt, that unity is the result of a divine organization—that the Church is the repository of the authority of Christ Himself—that she holds the faith once for all delivered to the saints, and has the Lord's promise that if she continues to do His will, she shall be led into all truth.

The difference is very wide between the servile and literal submission to a supposed infallible personal authority, and a conscientious carefulness to avoid whatever may come into collision with the received and recognized faith of the whole Church. The latter will be an influence no less powerful than the former to restrain the fleshly mind, and to bring the intellect into subjection. It will as completely repress all disposition to put forth theories and conceits, and thus tend to strengthen that unity of the spirit in which the perfection of the Church shall be attained. Thus it is that the objective unity of the Church is a means of bringing the intellect into subjection to the obedience of Christ.

But it is not only by authority that the Church is to act upon the intellect, and satisfy and perfect its development. The truth which is revealed by the Gospel must of necessity assume different aspects to different minds. The human and divine elements of Christianity—its objective and subjective sides—may easily array different parties in opposition to each other. Each is as sure of the truth as clear consciousness can make it, but each, while seeing its own side, has only half the truth, and can be only partially developed. It requires something more than philosophical argument or theological debate, to settle such questions in a way to satisfy the wants of minds that are confident of what they do hold and who see only antagonism in the other side. The intellect that is thus occupied by a half-truth, is imperfectly developed, and the imperfection must extend to every other faculty of the soul. Half-truths are the very life-blood of sectarianism; they are the most prolific source of controversies. The divided Church divides the truth, and one part is held by one section and another by another. Perfect development can only result from perfect truth, and hence the necessity that the Church shall be so constituted, that the whole truth as it is in Jesus shall be taught everywhere. And this cannot be done short of a universal organization, which shall harmonize every intellectual tendency, and satisfy every intellectual want—which shall furnish adequate nutriment for the analytic intellect of the East, and the synthetic tendency of the West—which shall alike meet the wants of the imaginative mind of the South, and the colder and less luxuriant temperament of the North. The opposition between the different tendencies can only then be seen to be not antagonism when each is made to supplement the other, and it is only under such conditions that the charity that rejoiceth in the truth can be completely satisfied. Earnest men will feel that it is right for them to contend against error, and so long as an opposite tendency appears to be an error will they fight against it. It is the office of a truly Catholic organization of the Church to bring opposite (not opposing) tendencies into harmony, and thus present the truth as one, that the intellect may be developed in its fulness, and all its various tendencies be met.

3. The necessity for some agency ordained of God to act upon the affections to bring them into subjection

to the will of God, is equally manifest. The heart is not to be controlled by abstractions. Something real and apprehensible by the senses is essential to shape the affections. The whole Gospel system, the manifestation of God in flesh, is in fact a divine arrangement for bringing the truth down to meet the finite and intelligible wants of men. The Church is just the embodiment of the system. Sacraments are ordained for bringing spiritual relations into the conditions of time and space. Christ Himself is indeed the true and chief object of the love and devotion of every one who believes on Him. Any love of the Church which supersedes the love of Christ is mere sectarianism, however pure the Church so loved may be.* But every one knows that the love of Christ manifests itself in the love of the brethren, in love for the mystical body of Him who is the personal object of devotion. The paraphrase of the 136th Psalm, which is such a favorite with all religious denominations—

"I love Thy kingdom, Lord," &c.,

is a form in which love to Christ is expressed more tangibly than by mere abstract declarations; and hence it is that these words, as well as the words of the Holy Ghost

* It is a remark of Coleridge, that he who begins by loving the Church more than he loves Christ, will go on to loving his own sect more than he loves the Church, and end with loving himself more than all. I quote from memory, but this is the substance, if not the exact form, of the utterance. It may be possible to love the Bride more than the Bridegroom, and even to the exclusion of the Bridegroom.

in the original, thrill through the soul of every devout Christian, with an energy that has its parallel only in the warmest natural affection or the most devoted patriotism. Such love is pure unselfishness. Love for the Church, or for what represents the Church, is one of the first dictates of a pure and elevated piety. "Even as Christ loved the Church, and gave Himself for it," so does love for the body of Christ possess the soul of every one in whom the love of Christ becomes controlling.

Now, it is manifest that, in order that this love may be pure, and continue so, its object must be real. It will be deep just as the body of Christ is discerned—just as the true relations between Christ and His Church are apprehended. This can only be when the whole company of the Baptized is seen as one. Under the influence or control of a sect, the sentiment of love for the Church is sure to become a narrow and selfish feeling—to degenerate into sectarian and partisan zeal—to want that pure and unselfish devotion which answers to the love of Christ for His Church. No sect can call forth the reverence and affection which should be inspired by the Bride of Christ—for the Bride is one, not made up of many. Only a largeness of charity, which comprehends all the baptized as brethren, which weeps over errors and faults, which avoids bitterness and strife, which longs for the removal of every hindrance to unity, which seeketh not its own, which rejoiceth not in iniquity but rejoiceth in the truth wherever seen, which beareth all things, believeth all things, hopeth all things, endureth all things—only such a love, extended to all the Baptized throughout the world, can answer to the true character of love for the Bride of Christ.

Such a love, sectarianism cannot beget; and if it springs up, is very apt to prevent and quench. Every sect has its existence based upon some narrow and exclusive principle; either some one or more dogmas held to the exclusion of all others, or some negation of a truth held in whole or in part by other portions of the baptized. The less there is of negation the greater the room for charity, and the less the hindrance to unity; but it is inevitable that, under the dominion of sectarianism, what should be the love for the Bride of Christ, degenerates into zeal for a sect, or else subsides altogether.

Since, then, an outward or objective organization is necessary to concentrate and form the spiritual affections which are involved in the attainment of Christian perfection and the perfect unity of the Spirit, it would seem that nothing less than a universal organization, embracing all the baptized, would answer the purpose. Even national Churches, organized on a principle of national independency, cannot develop the sentiment in its completeness: "In Christ Jesus there is neither Greek nor Jew, barbarian nor Scythian, bond nor free." National relations are of the flesh, and originate in man's fallen condition, and involve duties and attachments which are indhrances rather than otherwise to the spiritual development.

The time of the kingdom has not yet come, and until then nationalities must be kept in abeyance where spiritual relations are concerned. Anglicanism must involve more or less of English peculiarities, and the same is true with every other national Church organization, which stands upon its nationality.

The great results that the outward organization of the Church is designed of God to effect can only be secured by a truly Catholic constitution, which shall embrace under a universal government—what the form of that government should be, will be a subject of consideration hereafter—all those throughout the world who are members of the Body of Christ.* Under such conditions alone does the mind rise above the temporal and secular relations which spring from this present life. Then only do we realize that we are called to sit with Christ in the heavenlies, and that our citizenship is in heaven—that the Jerusalem which is above is the common mother of us all. Some such idea as this is implied in all the higher forms of spiritual sentiment, even in connection with sectarian organizations, but the tendency of sectarianism to crush and repress such sentiments is fearful and irresistible.

The effort is sometimes made to take a position of assumed superiority to all Church bonds—to cast off all sectarian or ecclesiastical influences; and such efforts are

* The authority of Christ cannot be felt when regarded as divided up among a number of coördinate yet independent sovereignties. No authority speaking and acting through a part and not being the expression of the whole can have absolute weight, or bind the conscience.

perhaps so far successful in individual cases, as to free individuals from the narrowness and selfishness which devotion to a sect inspires, and promote largeness and liberality towards others; but in such cases there is of necessity a failure in the subjection of the will and the intellect to the divine authority, and a general defect in character follows. Any organized attempts to cast off all ecclesiastical restraints, even the lowest and most nominal, as those of Congregationalism, uniformly result either in outright infidelity, or a more narrow and intense Sectarianism.

I have thus endeavored to show the necessity for an outward organization of the Church which shall be co-extensive with Christendom, for bringing the minds of baptized men into that state which shall fulfil the conditions of our Lord's Intercessory Prayer. Such an organization is necessary, to act upon those several powers and faculties in the man, by which his spiritual condition is determined. It must be used, unless we assume that all God's acts among men are to be direct upon his consciousness instead of by means of ordinances, which is contrary to all analogy and all revelation. Under these three heads of will, intellect, and affections, the whole man is comprehended, and by them the whole spiritual character is formed.

I am quite aware that, in assuming the existence of an outward unity as antecedent to the perfect unity of the Spirit, I am going counter to the prevalent opinion of Protestants, who generally will not allow that the outward organization is any thing but the result of the aggregation of those who believe, and consequently cannot regard it as the repository of authority. This is, I am persuaded, just the weak point of Protestantism—the point where it fails to apprehend the true relations of the Baptized to Christ. I repeat, therefore, the remark made at the beginning of this chapter—that the organization is before those who are added to it. The Church is in its constitution the New Jerusalem, and this the Apostle declares is "the mother of us all" (Gal. iv. 26). On Pentecost, by the descent of the Holy Ghost, the Lord established a spiritual polity—i. e., a polity of which the life and power is spiritual in distinction from natural, and every Christian has his standing as a baptized person derived from that polity. The preaching of the Word, by which we have been enlightened and converted, is a function of that body. The baptism whereby we have been grafted in, is another function. And so with all the nurture and discipline whereby the spiritual life has been strengthened. The offices of ministry, whether of the word or sacraments which men exercise, are not merely the works of individuals, but works of men as members of a body, and so are workings of the body. Although we may, without any fault of our own, have been separated from the mass of the baptized among whom a formal organization of the Church has had continuity, whatever grace or blessing we have received has been by virtue of the endowment which the Lord gave to His Church at Pentecost, which thus became the mother of all who are born to God. The recognition of this truth must precede any progress toward a recovered organic unity, by which the unity of Spirit can be restored and perfected.

The object at present to be hoped for is not so much the actual reunion of the several sects and portions of Christendom under one federative organization, as the constitution of a body which shall involve every principle of unity, by means of which the unity of the Spirit may be attained. This would not be effected by any recovery of intercommunion between national Churches, as for instance the Greek and Anglican, nor by any federative union of sects. No such union would act upon the spirits of members of the body in such a way as to bring every thought into subjection to the obedience of Christ. The hand of man in bringing it about would be too palpable to command the reverence and submission and love, which a new divine creation would call forth. The truce might be kept for a season, the treaty might be observed scrupulously, but the absence of the supernatural from it would leave it as a memory on every mind that it was a human treaty, after all.

God alone, by supernatural agency, can restore the unity of the Body of Christ.

CHAPTER III.

THE PRESENT STATE OF CHRISTENDOM CONSIDERED WITH REFERENCE TO UNITY.

The great schism between the East and West—The schism caused by the Protestant Reformation—This resulted not in dividing the Western Church into two great communities, but into a variety of National Churches, without any common headship—Subordinate divisions—Statement of the present condition of entire Christendom—The Church, in God's sight, embraces all the baptized—The question of lay baptism—The Church not now appearing as one whole, but existing in fragments—Principles upon which Unity may be recovered.

Before proceeding to consider the method of realizing the principles stated in the foregoing chapters, it will be well to dwell upon the present condition of Christendom, as related to the question we have in hand. This, it will be admitted, is widely different from what it was in the first, or even in the sixth, century. Schisms and heresies there were, but there was no settled division of the whole Christian community throughout the world, into distinct and opposing parties. With insignificant exceptions, the whole company of the baptized throughout the world constituted one community. True it is that there were disruptive causes at work in the midst of the Church—there were rivalries and animosities—there was strife and contention enough to drive into fragments any society which was not held together by some unseen power. The real and perfect bonds of unity were lost when the apostles ceased to be alive and rule the Church; but still there was enough of the conviction of the essential oneness of the body, and of the sin and evil of separation, to retain the various parts of the body together and prevent a permanent and irremediable schism.

The rivalry between the Eastern and Western Empires extended also to the Patriarchs of Rome and Constantinople, and thus the spirit of separation was encouraged, and nothing could be anticipated from the mutual curses and excommunications of the respective patriarchs, which were for several hundred years passing to and fro, but ultimate separation. The heart and spirit of the two communities had been divided and alienated upon grounds both of faith and of precedency. The last and crowning act which consummated the schism was the placing upon the altar of St. Sophia, by Leo IX., of the written decree of excommunication of the Eastern Patriarch, when his legates shook off the dust from their feet and departed forever. This was in the year A. D. 1054. The rupture of the Church was now complete. Other questions had separated men, and even communities, from the Church; but now schism divided the Church itself, and rent it in two.

The great schism of the eleventh century is the parent of all other schisms. The body being rent in twain, it is impossible to enforce the obligation to keep the unity of the Spirit.

The Western Church being separated from the Eastern, proceeded more and more, with the aid of the secular power, to consolidate her own organization, and was in the main successful. For four and a half centuries no disturbance of the organic unity of the Church in Western Europe occurred sufficient to effect a division. There were schisms within it, of which the long-standing schism of the Papacy in the fourteenth century is the most signal example; and this, no doubt, contributed very materially to prepare the way for the great Protestant schism. There were communities which dissented from some of the teachings of the Church, such as the Waldenses, and others like the followers of Huss in Bohemia, who, from demanding practical reforms in the Church, which were refused, were at length driven out of the Church and formed into separate associations; but until the times of Luther and the Protestant Reformation, there was no community of Christian people who separated themselves from the organic Roman Church by casting off the authority of its head. But in the sixteenth century this authority was more effectively questioned, and further schism occurred. The Protestants of the Continent denied the authority of the Papacy, and were cast off by it. The Church that was in England, acting under the lead of the English king, also separated herself from the organic unity of Rome. The Church in Scotland followed the course of the Continental Protestants. The Protestant schism was not, like the great schism of East and West, a division of the Western Church into two great parts, each having an organic unity of its own. While Rome retained her unity, the several Protestant nationalities were divided, each into a separate organization, having no common bond except their opposition to Rome. Each national Church was brought under the control of its national government. They were not organized alike. They had no common creed, no uniformity of worship, and were, in fact, so many separate communities, each having through its secular government a unity in itself, but having no unity together. The English Church retained the Episcopal organization, with the succession of the priesthood, liturgical services, and the sacramental doctrine. In Scotland, the Church was constituted on a Presbyterian basis. In Germany, France, Switzerland, Holland, etc., substantially the same organization was adopted, with such variations of doctrine and worship as the Calvinistic and Lutheran systems present. In the Northern nations the form of Episcopacy, though without the succession of priesthood, was established in connection with Lutheran doctrine.

The principle of objective unity being lost, when the power of the civil authority did not interpose there was nothing to hinder further subdivision, and so sects upon sects and schisms from schisms arose and multiplied. In Great Britain and in this country, the freedom from political restraint has favored the exercise of every form of belief and no belief, and consequently here we see as nowhere else the development of the sectarian principle, and (in this land at least) the unqualified assertion that sectarianism is a good thing.

It is no part of my present undertaking to decide where the blame of this state of things belongs. I have now only to state it in such form that we may, as from a height, look down upon the Christian world and behold its condition.

We have, then—

First. The Eastern Church, with its dependencies, including the Russian Church, which, in the main, constitute one community, not to speak of lesser communities in the East, of which our knowledge is but limited but which are substantially identified with it.

Secondly. The great Roman Catholic Communion, extending to all parts of the world, and bound into one, by the recognition of the authority of the Pope.

Thirdly. The great mass of Protestants, consisting of numerous communities, bound together by no common bond of unity, and some of them not recognizing the others as having any title to the Christian name.*

These several classes compose the company of the Baptized, or the visible Church militant, here upon earth.

Of all these classes, the Roman Catholic Church

* It is possible that these three divisions of Christendom constitute the "three parts" upon which the judgments announced in Rev. ch. viii. are poured out.

alone claims to be exclusively the Catholic Church, on the assumed ground that the Bishop of Rome, as the successor of St. Peter, is the divinely ordained head of the Church on earth. High Anglicans attempt to limit the comprehension of the Church to those who are in immediate relations to a pastorship of Apostolic Succession. The Baptists will allow none to be of the Church who are not immersed, but all other sects and parties are willing that all whom they can recognize as *evangelical*, which excludes Romanists and high Anglicans, should be regarded as comprehended within the Church. The Roman Catholics are the only party who maintain any principle of unity. The high Anglican is also a stickler for national independency, which is as fatal to Catholic unity as Congregationalism, while the very life of all other divisions is the asserted right of separation. Seen from a position in the heavenlies, the great community of the baptized must seem like a vast army divided into many parts, and, while not wholly regardless of their common enemy, yet much weakened and rendered powerless by contention among themselves. We cannot suppose that our Lord regards them otherwise than as one aggregate body. Among some portions of the whole His ordinances are preserved with a greater degree of perfection, and with others less, while some have so far departed from His ways as to have left scarce a shadow of His institutions among them, and to hardly have any title to be accounted His followers, and others have engrafted upon His ordinances a variety of human devices, which hinder and obscure what is divine. One portion has assumed a principle for unity which is a usurpation of His own prerogatives, and has been the fruitful cause of the present condition of the whole body; while others have so far lost sight of the true end of their calling as to repudiate all thoughts of unity.

Something may require to be said in defence of the principles of comprehension here assumed—viz., that the visible Church consists of all the Baptized. The Roman Catholic Church claims to be the possessor of the sole legitimate ecclesiastical authority, but even Romanists will allow that Protestants are by baptism their brethren, and in some way members of the same mystical body. The claim, therefore, for the possession of an exclusive divine authority does not preclude the admission that those who do not recognize that authority are members of the visible Church. The objection to our principle of comprehension comes most positively from high Anglicans and Episcopalians, who are much given to speaking of themselves as exclusively "the Church." Now, in England, where the English Church has an undoubted authority and an original mission, the claim to recognition of the establishment as The Church has a very strong basis, both as against dissenters, who have separated themselves from it, and the Church of Rome, which has intruded upon its field. In this land, the principles of Anglicanism, which are those of national independency (and even of diocesan independency), leave it no more claim than it can establish in the convictions of men. The Protestant Episcopal Church stands side by side with the Roman Catholic Church (not to speak here of other bodies), which has at least an equal right with itself to the title of the Church; for high churchmen will not deny that it has all the essentials of a Church. Now, the Roman Catholic Church has as good a right to extend itself as the English Church, and its orders and authority may be regarded, as far as the letter goes, of equal force. The Episcopal Church acquired no national standing under the colonial régime which would warrant it to claim the title of *the American Church*, at the occurrence of the Revolution. There were only a few scattered congregations of Episcopalians in the land, which were under the oversight of the Bishop of London; but no bishop had been sent here, and there was no ecclesiastical constitution, such as now prevails in the British colonies. The attempt, therefore, to assert for this body a standing in the religious world answerable to that of the established Church in England, is simply absurd. In some minds the talk of high churchmen about their Church as "The Church," provokes irritation; it may more properly be passed by with a smile. A certain class of high churchmen have undertaken to affirm that no baptism is to be regarded as real or valid, except what is administered by ministers who have received episcopal ordination; that is, that for the last three centuries there has been no baptism among Protestants outside of the Church of England and its offspring, and that consequently, the great mass of these communities are not to be regarded as belonging to the Church. This theory has indeed been sometimes carried to a most absurd application. This would be to admit that the energy of the Divine life would be just as effective outside the Church as within it. It cannot be denied that there have been at least as many and as abundant tokens of the operation of a supernatural grace among those outside of episcopacy as within it. It is a folly amounting to infatuation, to affirm that all the intellectual and moral manifestations produced among the Puritans and other dissenters in England, and among the Protestants in this country and on the Continent of Europe, are the results of mere nature, and not to be regarded in any way as fruits of the Spirit. Faith is the gift of God—the work of the Holy Ghost. When we see on a large scale evidences of an inwrought, effective faith—when we see whole communities under its power holding to the deepest mysteries of the Christian faith, such as the Trinity, the Incarnation, the Atonement, the work of the Holy Spirit—when we see manifest fruits of godliness, not only in individuals, but in the constitution of society, with whatever shortcomings and defects in matters ecclesiastical and ritual, and withal can give a very rational and consistent account of the rise, growth, and establishment of what may be anomalies in these systems—when such a state of facts presents itself to us, it is surely undervaluing by comparison the advantages and grace of Christian ordinances to say, that all these fruits have been attained in unbaptized communities.

It has certainly never, in the most palmy days of ecclesiastical authority, been maintained that baptism was void in its effect for want of regularity in the ordination of the administrator. Nay, the sanction expressly given to baptism by lay persons both male and female in circumstances of necessity, and the steady refusal of the Church to treat as void baptism administered by those in heresy or schism, provided the right matter and form were used, establishes the principle, so far as the action of the Church can do so, that baptism is not rendered void by want of regularity of ordination. Just such a state of facts as that occasioned by the Protestant Reformation had not indeed existed in the previous centuries. The schisms of the Donatists and Novatians, and other of the earlier sects, did not involve the rejection of the Episcopate, neither, on the other hand, was the rejection of the Episcopate regarded by the English Church as separating the reformed bodies of the Continent from the body of Christ, or denying the validity of baptism as administered among them.

The acts of separation from the communion of the Western Church having its head and centre at Rome, at the time of the Reformation, were not the acts of individual members. They were the acts of entire communities. The Church of an entire nation and people, acting as one, threw off that authority, and by so doing did not lose its corporate character. This was as true on the Continent as of the Church of England. The adoption on the Continent of an ecclesiastical system without the element of

Episcopacy was a distinct act. Now, where has there existed any authority to say that these bodies of Christian people, these national Churches, by this rejection of Episcopacy, separated themselves from the body of Christ? The authority of Rome has declared all Protestant bodies both heretical and schismatical, because of their rejection of the Papal authority and dogmas; but in this it places all Protestants, whether Episcopal or not, on a footing, and includes the Church of England with all the rest. The Church of England has never assumed to say that the want of Episcopacy separated any community from the body of Christ; and it is a mere exercise of private opinion in its worst form, for Episcopalians—or high Anglicans if they prefer the name—to assume to say that non-Episcopalians are not of the Church.

If these Protestant communities were not by the separation from Rome cut off from the body of Christ, and have not since then cut themselves off by rejecting the Christian faith, they still must have within them a measure of the supernatural grace which is inseparable from the body of Christ; and it is certainly not unreasonable to assume, that the principles which had been recognized as applicable to the case of baptism by unordained persons, may be admitted here, to establish the continuity of these bodies as members of the body of Christ, and their right to be regarded as important fragments of the one broken and divided body.

These remarks would not have their full application

to the various sects which have sprung up by individual separations from the original reformed Churches, which is the case of most of the sects in this land, inasmuch as these had no original corporate relations to the undivided Church. But as these sects have never been cut off by any competent authority, they are still to be regarded as component parts of the Church, while by the ordinance of baptism the power of continuity is retained.

The conclusion that we must reach upon such a review of the state of Christendom, is simply this: that the organization of the Church as one whole is dissolved—that the Church now exists in fragments, some having retained a greater and some a less portion of the truth which the Lord gave to her, and of the ordinances which He established for her perfecting. In a perfect condition, the Church, whole in every part, would give a perfect witness for all truth and every divine ordinance. But in her actual condition, the truth is divided among the several parts. The Roman Catholic Church has not ceased to witness for unity—for authority—for order—and to set forth, in however perverted a form, doctrines and usages which are essential constituents of the perfect truth as it is in Jesus. But she has closed the Bible, and overlaid divine truth and order with doctrines and commandments of men, and usurpations of authority. Protestants, on the other hand, have with one voice contended for the exercise of the individual conscience and the private judgment, for the open Bible and the reasonable service, while in doing so they have erred to the extent of throwing off all authority, and disregarding all order, and abusing the right of private judgment into rationalism and unbelief.

Among Protestants, again, the Church of England has continued to witness to the reality of a divine ministry in the Church, to order in worship, to the reality of sacraments, while, for the greater part of her separate existence, she has practically failed to recognize the reality of a divine supernatural life in ordinances; and this has been the cause of the separation from her of various sects, who have sought in separation to attain what she failed to supply.

A similar division of the truth among the different sects is seen in the case of the Calvinistic and Methodist Churches, the one so grasping the divine side of the mystery of united divine and human agency in salvation, and the other the human side, as to give a half truth to each, and leave space for constant misunderstanding and confusion.

The view we have taken of the condition of the universal Church, and the relation of the parts to the whole, suggests the principles upon which unity may be recovered:

1. The unity we are to contemplate and hope for, must comprehend all parts of the scattered and broken body. It must be a unity which shall include Roman Catholics, and Greeks, and Armenians, and Protestants—which must extend over the whole of Christendom. It is not merely the reconciling of Protestant sects one with

another, for the purpose of a stronger and more effectual assault against Rome, nor an intercommunion of the Greek and Episcopal Churches for the same purpose. This would only intensify the sect spirit, transferring it from the narrower to the wider field, and would not tend in any degree to illustrate to the world the unity of the Father and the Son.

2. It is manifest that no unity by the union of sects, or of national Churches, is possible.

If all other bodies of Christians could by some arrangements and concessions be united into a confederation, still the Roman Catholic Church would by its first principles be excluded. No one will be so enthusiastic as to suppose that that communion will ever surrender its claims to universal supremacy. Neither is the Eastern Church at all likely to abandon the ground it has held for so many centuries, and admit the supremacy of Rome. It is hardly necessary to say, that it is equally impossible for the Protestant sects to surrender their hostility to that branch of Christendom. Neither can the Protestant sects be blended into one body organically united. But, it is needless to make any statements on this point, so obvious are the facts in the case. In fact, such unity is disavowed by many who are now engaged in the discussion of the subject.

3. It is plain that the restoration of unity must be a work of divine power. It will require the operations of a grace more special and abundant than we now witness in connection with the received ordinances of the

Church, to fit into a living unity, so that they may be one as the Father and the Son are one, the separated and scattered members of the body of Christ. It must be the result of a revival of spiritual life—an extraordinary outpouring of the Holy Spirit, which shall enlighten the minds of baptized men, to see the oneness of their hope and faith and obedience—to cast aside all their sectarian preferences, and submit themselves with one mind and one heart to the authority of Christ the Lord.

4. A restored unity must proceed from a centre or nucleus, which shall originate in some supernatural divine actings recognized as authoritative; which centre shall gather around it, first those members of the body who shall be found willing to be gathered into a unity and to be moulded collectively into the perfect image of Christ, so that the perfect man may be brought forth. The realization of unity does not require that all shall be gathered, for there are many among the baptized who will, doubtless, reject the counsel of God toward them. What is required is, that there shall be a body, in which the true unity of the Spirit can be realized. The existence of such a body on earth will be to all men a test of their willingness to be carried on to perfection. They who refuse this test will either be found among the followers of Antichrist, or else will suffer in the tribulation which his reign of iniquity will bring upon all who will be faithful to the truth. But the purpose of God will be accomplished, to have a body, in which all the members are united one to another in the perfect unity of the Spirit.

The members of this body will be gathered out of all sects—all parties—all fragments of Christendom. Through the operation of the Holy Ghost, they will be enlightened and moulded into one. No sect or fragment, however great its extent, can be made this centre, for that would be to give to one part the honor which belongs only to the whole, and to give a sanction to the claims of that sect, and an authentication of its errors and defects.

All must admit that here is a *nodus vindice dignus*—a case that will warrant a divine interposition, and it is not beyond what we may reasonably expect, to hope that God will arise and put to His hand, to remove a difficulty which no human wisdom can reach, and which none of the institutions recognized among men have hitherto had power to clear away.

Thus we have the facts and conditions of the problem. Let us now pass to consider what we can learn regarding the method of its solution.

CHAPTER IV.

THE RECOVERY OF ORGANIC UNITY

Unity can only be restored by Supernatural Action—The Original Planting of the Church—The Rise of the Ecclesiastical System—Necessity felt for some Ordinance for Preserving Unity—Culminating at last in the Papacy—No Conventional Authority sufficient—The only possible Solution, the Supernatural Appointment of Men with Apostolic Powers—Does the New Testament warrant any such expectation—How it would be done.

I HAVE said that the only means of recovering unity, is by the establishment through supernatural action, of a centre of unity around which those of the baptized who are found willing to be moulded into the unity of the Spirit may be gathered. Any such movement must have a supernatural initiative, otherwise it would be a human work and not an object of faith. As claiming our recognition, moreover, it must be in harmony with what we learn from Holy Scripture, and with God's past actings in His Church. We may not look for the establishment of a "new Church," such as Swedenborg attempted, for that would be to assume that the Church in this dispensation had come to an end, and virtually to say, as he does, that the Resurrection was past already. The Church restored in unity must be the same body which was formed at Pentecost, inheriting the same promises, in which the life then imparted by the Holy Ghost has through Baptism had an unbroken continuity. The restored unity must consist of the members of that same body taken as they are—not baptized anew, and gathered into one by the operation of the Holy Ghost. The principles, too, upon which the Church is to be restored in unity, must be those which we learn from the New Testament were in operation at the beginning of this dispensation. For we cannot expect a new revelation; we must be taught out of that which we have received, and whereby Christendom is to be judged. Even as when Adam fell, God did not destroy the fallen race and create a new one, but provided for its recovery by a new creation in the Incarnate Word, so is the Church to be restored to its unity, not by destruction of that which has fallen away and the calling into existence of a new body, but by taking the members of the existing body, and through the outpouring of the Spirit reëstablishing among them that perfect order from which the Church has fallen, thus preserving its identity.

To obtain light on this subject let us then revert to the original planting of the Church.

The Church at the first was all contained in the apostolic college. To the twelve was the charter of the Church given, not for themselves individually, but as the Church. To them was the Holy Ghost first given, and by their apostolic action was it imparted to others. By their preaching and the power of the Holy Ghost, men were saved and joined themselves to the apostles, and continued steadfastly in their fellowship. They constituted a centre, around which the Church as a body was formed. The first local organization was, of course, the Church in Jerusalem. As the Gospel extended, other Churches were formed in Antioch, in Samaria, in Corinth, in Ephesus, in Rome, and to the utmost parts of the earth. All these several local churches constituted but one society, of which the connecting link was the apostolic college. These churches thus united were collectively the Church of God—the Body of Christ. As respects each other, the several churches were independent—and here is the grain of truth in the theory of congregationalism; but as respects the whole body, they were bound into one by their common subordination to the authority of Christ in His apostles. There was not one local Church, as that of Jerusalem, claiming to be the root or trunk of which all the rest were branches. No Church claimed to be the mother and mistress of all churches. Christ was the vine, the stock, the trunk, and the churches were branches in Him. The authority of the Lord in His apostles was the cementing link of the whole. This was the "bond of peace" by which all were held together. Subjection to this made the whole to be one body. So long as the apostles lived, there could be no doubt or question as to where the bond of unity lay. As Churches continued in the "Apostles' fellowship," so were they in fellowship with one another; and, as St. John writes in his first epistle (chap. i. 3), as they were in fellowship with the apostles, they were in fellowship with the Father and the Son.

Such was the unity of the whole Church.

The unity of the local church was secured by the appointment of one of the elders to preside over the rest, upon whom rested the responsibility and oversight of the whole.*

After the death of the apostles, a further effort to secure unity on a larger scale resulted in the appointment of Metropolitans, and ultimately of Patriarchs, of which in the early Church there were, according to Bingham, in the fourth century thirteen, but of which the number was at length reduced to four, viz.: Rome, Antioch, Constantinople, and Alexandria. These are simply historical facts, and their significance is this: that in the centuries directly following the apostolic age, in the absence of Apostles the Church felt the necessity for some ordinance for the preservation of unity—for keeping the whole Christian community together. There was an instinct of unity in it which resisted the disintegrating tendency, by conceding to the chief pastors in the principal cities of the empire, an authority over the surrounding churches. For the local, the Metropolitical, and the Patriarchal sees, this arrangement furnished a bond of unity for the churches within their respective

* Οι καλως προεστωτες πρεσβυτεροι (1 Tim. v. 17). This evidently refers to the elders who in the several churches were placed over their brethren as presidents; *i. e.*, were made bishops—called in the Apocalypse "angels." It is strange that men of learning should cite this text as a scriptural warrant for what are by Presbyterians called *Ruling Elders*

territories. The cases of Timothy and Titus, who were sent by St. Paul to exercise authority over the churches in and around Ephesus and Crete, suggest the probability that this subordination to Metropolitans and Patriarchs was not without apostolic sanction. As such it would have weight and force upon the conscience in a way that no conventional arrangement could do. But there was for centuries no authority claimed or exercised over the whole Church, until, after the conversion of Constantine, first the Emperor, and afterwards the Bishop of Rome assumed that authority. The earliest exercise of universal authority was by the Emperor.* From him it passed over, so far as the Western Church was concerned, to the Pope. The acquiescence of the whole Church east and west in the supremacy of the Emperor, and of the Western Church in that of the Pope, shows that there was a conviction in the mind of Christendom of the need of a central authority to bind the Church together into one.

Still, any authority that is merely conventional, self-imposed, and not recognized as absolutely *jure divino*, will fail to produce perfect results even in those who acknowledge it; and for this reason, that the recognition of it does not proceed from faith. The ecclesiastical system which has a conventional origin can only control the rational judgment of men, and when it ceases to do that, its power is gone. The secret of the power which the Church of Rome exerts over its members lies in the conviction it has been able to produce, that the Pope is

* In a later chapter I shall furnish some illustrations of this fact.

the successor of Peter in the See of Rome, and as such has received from the Lord an indefeasible authority over the whole Church, which it is deadly sin to question or resist. However mistaken this is on the part of Roman Catholics, an act of faith. The Church is identified with the Papacy as a divinely planted institution, which may not be set aside, and which as such has the promise and assurance of infallibility. The effect of this belief upon the conscience is as powerful as though it rested upon an actual revelation, and it is thus to that body the bond of unity. It is only when the moral results of the Papal system suggest doubts of its having a divine authority that there can be any shaking of the allegiance which is felt to be due to a truly divine ordinance.

In order, then, to the recovery of a unity by which the whole Church throughout the world may be bound into one universal or Catholic organization, there must be a central authority which can be received and respected as being placed and endowed by Christ Himself —an authority such as that by which the Church at the beginning was constituted one body.

How, then, can this authority be brought into existence? It may not be conventional, or originated by the agreement of men or churches one with another. It may not, as the papacy did, grow out of the grants of authority which the churches conceded, first to Metropolitans and then to Patriarchs. It must come from above. It can proceed only from supernatural actings of God the Father and the Lord Jesus Christ. It must have its hold upon the faith of the Church. In plain words, the only possible solution of the problem of unity is, the supernatural appointment of men with apostolic authority and apostolic powers, who shall enter into the ministry and possess the endowments of the Apostles who were at the beginning, to whom the Lord said, "As my Father hath sent me, so send I you;" "Lo, I am with you all days, even to the consummation of the age."

Such a ministry, and no other, will furnish a centre of unity around which all may gather who are willing to be gathered into a unity. The recognition of it will furnish a restraint upon the wills and the intellects of men, whereby the spirit of obedience and of teachableness will be exercised, and men may become like little children. Being received by faith and apprehended by spiritual discernment, it will give exercise to the spiritual nature, and will repress the sharp logical tendency which excites self-conceit and hardens the heart from the exercise of charity.

Such a ministry of Apostleship would, from its endowment of divine wisdom, be qualified to decide all doubtful questions of doctrine, and thus remove one of the existing causes of division, while the recognition of it as a supreme central authority, having the mind of Christ and led by His Spirit, will preclude all rivalries and contentions among different Churches. It would be qualified by its supernatural endowment, not only to prescribe the true order of divine worship, but also so to instruct, that men's prejudices may be removed, and they be made willing to dwell together as brethren in unity.

Is there any warrant in the New Testament for the expectation of such a favor? To me it seems very clear. St. Paul says, "God hath set Apostles first in the Church." This implies that the Apostolic office proper is an essential part of her constitution, without which she cannot be complete; and surely we may look to God to give whatever shall be necessary to make perfect the Bride of His Son. The promise of the Lord, "Lo, I am with you," etc., also implies that there is no time when the Church may not hope to receive from Him the gift of Apostleship. Apostleship comprehends all other ministries, and the words of the Lord constitute a promise to the Church of all the fulness of ministry in men, which she may need at any time during this dispensation.

It will not be difficult to understand how such a ministry may be raised up of God, if we fully recognize Christ as the living Head of the Church at the Right hand of the Father. In sending forth His Apostles before His ascension, He did not abdicate His right to interfere directly in the affairs of His Church at any and at all times. Nay, the promise of His presence with the Church, implies that he may exercise His prerogative to send forth whom He may choose at any and at all times. This right certainly was exercised in the case of Paul, whom He called from the heavens, and sent him forth with a power and authority equal to that of the first twelve; and what He did then He may do again. The ordinary way of God's acting in the Church is by ordinances. No man has any right to assume, that he can individually obtain any grace or spiritual benefit from God, except through the ordinances of divine appointment. To expect any thing else is fanaticism, which can result only in evil. But God is not so tied to His own ordinances that He may not in exigencies act without them. When that ordinance in which all other ordinances are concentrated has lapsed, it is not fanaticism to expect that He may interpose to restore that ordinance that His Church may be complete. This ordinance of Apostleship is not a secondary, but a primary one. It comes not into existence through the agency of any other ordinance. Apostles are not of man, neither by men, but by Jesus Christ and God the Father (Gal. i. 1). God may make men to be Apostles, and give assurance to the Church of their calling in such form as shall justify the Church in receiving them as sent by the Lord.

Such an act of God, as supernatural and extraordinary, would indeed make a demand upon our faith. It would be an acting that would partake of the miraculous; but it will be admitted by every one who adequately considers the subject, that unity cannot be restored without miracle. There are no means now in operation for effecting unity, and its recovery cannot be looked for without a supply of means adapted to the end. If the means are not in operation, they must be supplied from on high; they must come in an extraordinary way. Can any one, who admits that the Church is a divine creation—a supernatural organization, in which, through ordinances and sacraments, there is a constant flowing forth of supernatural life, deny the possibility of an extraordinary operation of supernatural power to effect such a grand result as that of unity? Is it too much to hope for, that God the Father, and the Lord Jesus Christ, should provide means and ordinances whereby the Holy Ghost, dwelling in the Church, may work in the hearts of the faithful to knit them into one, and thus fulfil the petitions of the Lord's intercessory prayer?

The restoration of a ministry endowed with the authority that was at first conferred upon apostles, and with the grace needful to make that authority effectual, would completely supply the want. Here would be a centre for the entire Christian world, by the recognition of which all the baptized may be united into one. Here would be an authority by which open questions may be settled, and unruly and ambitious wills may be brought into subjection, or cut off as useless branches from the vine.

The statement has been made, and there are many, doubtless, who would be ready to assert it, that no institution can be recognized as a means of unity which has not had an unbroken continuity in the Church from the beginning. This would be to affirm that the Church can never have lost or forfeited any of the grace that was conferred upon her at the first. And yet, so far as principles go, the statement may, to a certain extent, be admitted. For the greater part of the time that has elapsed since the history of the Church began, the necessity of some ministry answering to the apostolic has been felt, and a substitute for it has been recognized. It was seen in the fourth century that some authority was needed that should be universal in its scope; and in the absence of any proper ecclesiastical authority, the Emperors assumed universal supremacy. Only the felt necessity of a ministry of apostolic powers, could have rendered possible the ascendency which the Bishops of Rome acquired and attempted to exert over the whole of Christendom. For centuries past, Rome has been known as the *Apostolic See*, and it has been claimed to be the inheritor of all apostolic, as distinguished from episcopal, powers. The idea, then, of an apostolic ministry is not a new one, nor is the belief in its necessity as a bond of unity. It has not been recognized in the English Church for three centuries past, it is true (and it is from this quarter that the objection proceeds), but England is a small part of Christendom, and the voice of the English Church has had no great weight in these centuries as an authority in such matters.

The way in which unity would be restored by such an agency would be, not by drawing different churches and sects together and compromising their difficulties, but by gathering out of all churches those who were prepared to receive such a grace, and knitting them into a perfect unity by spiritual bonds. Such would form a nucleus, in which the true principles of unity could be exemplified, and around which might ultimately be gathered all who should desire to be delivered from the city of confusion which Christendom has become. Thus would the Lord have on earth a body in which the unity of the Father and the Son—the true unity of the Spirit—could be seen, and by which He might save and gather into one all who would be willing to be saved, so that we may all come into the unity of the faith and of the knowledge of the Son of God unto a perfect man. Thus would the desire expressed in our Lord's prayer be fulfilled, and the end be attained of having on this earth a body perfectly constituted in unity—a "Church without spot or wrinkle, or any such thing, holy and without blemish"—prepared to be translated and to be presented to the Lord at His coming, as a bride adorned for her husband.

It would not follow that such a ministry supernaturally supplied would be at once recognized and received even by all true Christians. Its recognition would be a test of the faith and obedience of men—of their willingness to be freed from the narrow bonds of sectarianism, and to be gathered together into one. Not without trial and judgment would the gathering be effected. The churches would need to feel the pressure of the rising power of Antichrist before they would so realize the need of a common bond as to be willing to receive a supernatural visitation; for schism has defiled and polluted the entire Church, and there is no portion of it that is willing to be made a living sacrifice. "All seek their own, not the things that are Jesus Christ's."

I have stated this matter hypothetically, and believe it to be the only method by which the problem of a recovered unity can be solved. But it is not mere hypothesis: the hypothesis is derived from existing facts. There has been for thirty years past a spiritual work in progress, in which this theory—so to call it—has been realized. In the year of grace, 1830, God in answer to the prayers of many of His faithful people, who sought from Him a reviving in His Church, was pleased to pour out His Spirit in Scotland and other parts of the British Isles, by which the gifts of the Holy Ghost were revived, especially the gift of prophecy attended by some striking cases of miraculous healing. They who received these gifts, and others who recognized them, were led by the words of the Holy Ghost thus spoken to pray earnestly to God to send Apostles to His Church. In the year 1832 this prayer began to be answered by the supernatural calling (somewhat after the manner in which Paul and Barnabas were called in Antioch, Acts ch. xiii.) of first one, and then another among those who believed in those things, to be Apostles, until the complete number of twelve were thus called, and in 1835 they were solemnly separated to their work.

Since that time they have been fulfilling their ministry, and by them churches have been formed in different parts of Europe and America, in which the principle of unity has been developed, and every form of truth which has at any time found expression in the universal Church, has been recognized and set forth. The Apostolic College is a central authority—a CATHOLIC SUPREMACY, which binds into one all the several churches which acknowledge them, in Great Britain, Germany, Holland, Switzerland, Canada, and the United States, and wherever believers are found. In these churches every thing that is essential to the perfect unity of the Spirit is maintained—absolute uniformity in doctrine, and harmony in all teaching—uniformity as to all the essentials of worship, identity in the form of organization, and of ministry as far as the materials are at hand. All are "perfectly joined together in the same mind and in the same judgment."

The system has been long enough in operation to test its capabilities. It does not preclude the entrance of all evil. It does not restrain men absolutely from sin, and from apostacy from the Church—this cannot be in the natural body—but it has shown its capacity for throwing off every opposing element, and for subduing, with none but spiritual agencies, the wills of men into subjection to an authority which is the authority of the Lord. The Apostleship, being the divine ordinance for the guidance of the Church into all truth, is looked to as the determiner of questions of serious doubt that might, in the hands of inferior ministers, occasion strife and dissension. Apostles do not assume to be "Vicars of Christ," nor does any one Apostle act on a question of universal concern without his brethren. The unity of the Lord's rule is made manifest by being vested in a definite number, which can act as one, and acts not unless all are agreed together as to what they shall ask for, and what shall be decreed.

It falls not within the range of my present undertaking to enter into a history of this work, or a detail of the organization effected by it. I refer to it in this connection as a demonstration of the practicability of the method which has been herein laid down. The assertion of a title to Apostleship, of course, needs some signs to prove its warrant. Nothing can more effectually do this than the fruits of thirty years' labors. These, I affirm, show the possibility of a recovered unity by means of a supernatural divine acting. They show what may be done if the faithful servants of Christ—those who truly believe in Him and love Him—will but consent to lay aside their sectarian prejudices, and admit the reality of His rule in the Church, and submit themselves to Him. There is already a body sufficiently large, known as the "Catholic Apostolic Church"—by which name is to be understood, not that it claims that title exclusively, but that it refuses to be called by any other—to make it clear what it might be if it were larger in respect to numbers, and wide enough in its extent, to show that it might embrace the whole of Christendom. It is a standing proof of the possibility of a Catholic Church—of a universal organization without the evils of the Papacy. It is a standing witness against the confusion of Babylon—the Sectarianism of the present age.

It is the solution of the problem how unity may be restored.

CHAPTER V.

THEORIES OF UNITY.

The Episcopal theory of Unity, that the collective Episcopate is the Bond of Unity—But what is to unite the Bishops, who have been the chief agents of Schism?—Geneneral acknowledgment of Episcopacy by Protestant sects would not unite them with Rome, nor with the East.

We have already considered the theory of unity which is entertained by the greater part of the Christian communities which have resulted from the Protestant Reformation, viz.: that the only unity that is to be looked for is a unity of spirit which allows of the existence of sects, and has no corresponding organization. Into this view the Episcopalians of the low church school, I believe, enter for the most part.

Another view is that held by the Episcopalians of the high church school, which is known as Anglicanism, viz.: that the unity of organization in the Church consists in the collective episcopate, by which, as by a grand chain reaching down from the beginning and extending throughout the world, the whole Church is bound into a corporation, while different national churches are so many distinct and coördinate branches of the one body—the peculiarity of the theory being the denial of any ministry for uniting the whole company of bishops into one organization, or any head of the episcopate.

A third theory is that of the Papacy, which affirms that the one Church must be united under one head, and that the bishop of the Church of Rome, as the successor of St. Peter, is the divinely appointed head of the universal Church.

A few pages will be devoted to the consideration of these two last named theories.

The collective episcopate extends over the whole of Christendom, embracing the heads of all the local or diocesan churches throughout the world. The churches respectively are united in their bishops: but how are the bishops united? It is idle to say the bishops are united by their ordination, or apostolic succession, and that this is the bond of unity. As well might the common union which all Christians have in their baptism be adduced as the complete bond of unity. All Christians are one as members of the one body, and all bishops are one as members of the one episcopate, and all priests are one as members of the one priesthood; but the oneness of the members of the episcopate no more fulfils the idea of unity which the Church is to attain, than does the oneness of the membership by baptism. The bishops of the East and the West are not united, though both alike are members of the collective episcopate; neither are the bishops of the Roman and Anglican Churches. Nay, even intercommunion, as between the Episcopal churches in England and America, where there is no common organization, does not constitute unity. Much less is the possession of the common episcopate, when the churches are at variance, the bond of unity. Who have been the prime agents in the schisms that have rent Christendom asunder? Who are the parties primarily and directly in antagonism? Are they not the bishops? Who have been the leaders in the earlier, and, as respects the great schism, the lesser schisms which occurred in the East? Were they not the bishops? Who were the prime contestants in the long-protracted quarrels which produced the great schism? Were they not the Patriarchs of Rome and of Constantinople, representing the archbishops and bishops subject to them respectively? Might not an objector to the Episcopal order say that the laity had nothing to do with these controversies, and that but for the ambition and strife of their prelates the schism would never have occurred? What but the ambition of the Roman Pontiffs, sustained by their subject bishops on the one hand, and the refusal of the Eastern bishops to own the supremacy of the Roman Church on the other, has prevented the healing of that schism to the present hour? Would the acknowledgment of the episcopate by the non-Episcopal Churches be a restoration of Catholic unity? Would not the Episcopal churches be as much as ever divided from the Church of Rome? The episcopate needs a universal headship—a centre—as much as the body of the baptized. The question still recurs: *Quis custodiet custodes?* Who shall unite the bishops, so as to cause them to preserve the unity of the

Spirit? to be one as the Father and the Son are one? to bring them to be perfectly joined together in the same mind and in the same judgment? How is it in the purely Episcopal churches—those of England and America—which have a common episcopate? Is unity perfect among them? Are they agreed in point of doctrine? What say the various parties of high and low Anglicans, Evangelicals, Broad Church? Is the influence of the episcopate such as to lead the people on to the unity of the faith, and of the knowledge of the Son of God? Do not the doctrinal and practical differences that exist between bishops and clergy of different schools declare that the knowledge of the Son of God among them comes far short of that perfection which is implied in Unity?

In truth, this theory can only be maintained on the ground upon which Congregationalism is defended—that there is required no visible ordinance for unity. It is only Congregationalism on a large scale—the congregations being in this case dioceses headed up in bishops, instead of local churches personally represented. The principle which requires Episcopacy as the bond of unity for the local church, can only be logically complete when applied to the universal Church, and the denial of the necessity of a bond of unity for the universal Church cannot logically stop short of its denial in relation to the local church.

These then are facts—that the collective episcopate does not operate as a bond of peace, holding Christendom together in such manner as to exercise and develop the unity of the Spirit, and that the members of the collective episcopate have been the principal agents in causing the divisions of Christendom.

Nor would it be any different if the episcopal principle were universally restored by the dissolution of the Papacy, or by the non-episcopal bodies adopting Episcopacy. This must be said for the Papacy, that it restrains the tendency to schism, which, without it, would break out afresh, and aggravate what now prevails.

CHAPTER VI.

THE ROMAN DOCTRINE OF UNITY.

The Roman Church has always witnessed to Unity—Two distinct Ideas—Catholic Unity and the form of its Realization—Papal arguments—The Primacy of Peter—What it involved—His position compared with that of Paul—A Primacy in the Apostolic College necessary that they might act as one—Arguments of R. J. Wilberforce examined—The Bishop of Rome did not inherit Peter's primacy—What is the amount of the distinction that the early Fathers ascribe to the See of Rome—The Primacy of Peter a different thing from the Supremacy of the Popes—Admitted by Roman Catholic writers—Ffulkes on the Divisions of East and West—The first acts of Supremacy exerted by Constantine and his successors.

Of all the several parts into which Christendom is divided, the only one that has maintained the true idea of Catholic unity, is that which is united under the Bishop of Rome. This, no doubt, has ever been, and is still, the secret of her great strength and durability. It is a superficial philosophy which can be satisfied with asserting that the entire system of the Papacy is false—that there are no divine principles involved in it. It has become an axiom with all thinking persons, that no system ever took and kept a strong hold upon a large part of mankind which had not in it elements of truth. When, therefore, we are called upon to meet and counteract the influence of any system of institutions, which we are persuaded is, on the whole, contrary to truth, the first step to any successful conflict is to discover and eliminate the elements of truth which it contains, so that what remains may be the more unsparingly and rigorously assailed. There are several distinct forms of truth to which the Roman Church has at all times given witness, more steadily than has been done by any other portion of divided Christendom. She has the deep things of God which have been by perversion made to be the "depths of Satan;" but we must beware lest, in our hatred of the perversion, we also reject the truth.

One of the truths to which the Roman Church has continued to give a witness is that of unity—the unity of the whole Christian body under one organization. This is the truth; the error which has been the parent of many other errors which pervade the actual Roman system is, that the headship of the Catholic Church is by divine authority vested in the Bishop of Rome. It is very manifest that here are two ideas which we may regard separately. The idea of unity is one thing, the form of its realization another. Assuming, as is done in this discussion, the truth of Catholic unity, there remains the inquiry what there is to support the Roman doctrine of the form in which it is realized.

In a discussion of this nature this question could not be well passed over. Still I do not purpose to go into any exhaustive examination of it, nor to enter upon any original investigations of its history or progress. I shall make use mainly of the statements and admissions of writers in the Roman Catholic interest. The two authors to whom I propose to refer are, R. J. Wilberforce, formerly Archdeacon in the English Church, in his work on the "Principle of Church Authority," written as an apology for his secession to Rome, and a recent work entitled, "The Divisions of Christendom on East and West, by Edmund S. Ffulkes, formerly fellow and tutor of Jesus College, Oxford." This latter work seems to be written in the hope of preparing the way for renewed efforts for the restoration of unity, and while fully in the interest of Rome, yet makes a frank admission of the facts which serve as an apology for the divisions which the author hopes to contribute to healing. There can be no better sources of reference than such authors. They are men whose adhesion to the Papacy is not the result of education, but has come from the consideration of arguments which they place in the strongest light in which they can be put.

The first link in this chain of argument—the staple from which it all hangs, is the primacy of Peter in the Apostolic College. This I must admit. All that is said of and to Peter by our Lord, and by the writers of the New Testament, cannot pass for nothing. Peter was, in one sense, the "Rock" on which the Church was built. He was the First—as stated by St. Matthew (ch. x. 2)—and that not merely in the order of his calling—in which he was not first apparently, but as a *primus inter pares*. There is something significant in our Lord's words to him. "Satan hath desired to have you, that he might sift you as wheat: but I have prayed for *thee*, that thy faith fail not: and when thou art converted, strengthen thy brethren" (Luke xxii. 32). The charge which the Lord gave to him after the Resurrection, "feed my lambs, feed my sheep," cannot be supposed to be devoid of some special significance. When Paul went to Jerusalem, he went "to see Peter." All this implies some positive relation to the rest of the Apostles. It may well be called a *primacy*, and it remains to inquire what is involved in it.

I cannot accede to Wilberforce's notion, that Peter, as distinguished from his brethren, "was to be associated by peculiar copartnership in one of the functions of his master, and become by grace that which Christ was by nature." This is a theory without a shadow of Scriptural warrant, and is a bold assumption upon which to build up the theory of the Papacy. The real significance of the distinction of Peter is, doubtless, what was asserted by the early writers, that the unity of the Apostolate might be represented in him. The twelve were to act as one, and so the charge was given to one for all, that there might be no divisive action. In this view it may be admitted as possibly true, though it certainly cannot be proved from the New Testament, that Peter's assent and approval was requisite to the efficiency of the united action of the Apostolic college, though there is no ground at all for what Wilberforce claims (p. 172), "that the coöperation of no other individual was necessary to him." His primacy could not make him independent of his brethren. The Apostolate was represented in Peter, and was thus constituted into a twelve-fold unity, but there is no evidence that farther than this there was any function, or any prerogative belonging to him, which was not equally exercised by all the rest.

But while it is admitted that Peter held such a primacy among his fellow apostles to the circumcision, what shall be said of the relations of Paul? Clearly he was not subordinate to Peter. He himself declares he was "not a whit behind the very chiefest of the Apostles" (2 Cor. xi. 5), and it is evident that he held a position analagous to Peter's. This is a point that has been very much overlooked, and needs explaining. Peter was the head of an organized apostleship who were sent to the Jews. Paul calls himself "the Apostle of the Gentiles." The Apostleship of the Gentiles was committed to him, as the Apostleship of the Circumcision was to Peter. These words define his position.* Whatever position Peter held in the one case, Paul held in the other. If Peter were the Primate of the apostles to the Jews, Paul was Primate in the Apostleship of the Gentiles. Wilberforce gives one citation in which this view of the respective relations of the two apostles is expressly declared. He says (p. 164): "Hilary the deacon says: 'Paul mentions Peter alone, and compares him to himself because he had received a primacy for the founding

* He received a distinct commission involving all the gifts that had already been bestowed, and which were involved in Apostleship, and also whatever specialty belonged to Peter.

of the Church, while he himself was elected in like manner to have a primacy in founding the churches of the Gentiles.'" Again: "As he assigns associates to Peter, namely, the illustrious men among the apostles, so he joins Barnabas to himself, who had been associated with him by divine appointment; yet he claims the grace of the Primacy as granted by God to himself alone, as to Peter alone was it granted among the apostles."

The principle of a Primacy—a First from whom unity might proceed, and by whom the Twelve were bound into one, which was first exemplified in Peter, was further exemplified in Paul. He had an office, the same in its nature as was Peter's, but a ministry which was entirely distinct. But he had a distinct and moré advanced revelation than Peter's, which he calls "my gospel," and which he declares he was taught by special revelation, not having received it through the medium of Peter or his brethren (Gal. i. 11, 12); and he went up to Jerusalem "to see Peter," because it was necessary that there should be a perfect understanding between the two apostleships. Peter was not primate with respect to him, but only with respect to his fellow Apostles to the Circumcision. Paul's primacy was not so distinctly called into exercise, because he had not associated with him a full number of apostles. He speaks of himself as an *εκτρωμα* (1 Cor. xi. 7), a premature birth, the meaning of which is, that the time had not arrived for the Church to bring forth from her womb the fully formed Apostleship to the Gentiles; but in order to the revelation of the purpose of God in the Gentiles, it was necessary that one should be thus early, prematurely called forth to inaugurate the Gentile Church, and commit to it the revelation which was not made to the Church of the Circumcision; which apostleship was to come out in its completeness in the end of the dispensation. A Primacy in Paul, therefore, has the same effect as a Primacy in Peter, and this dignity was not a prerogative peculiar to that apostle.

A Primacy in the apostolic college was requisite to the unity of the Apostolate, inasmuch as no collective body can act without a head; and the scriptural fact of the primacy of Peter is the standing answer to the theory that the visible Church can be bound in unity without a visible centre of unity. Here is a reason sufficient to justify all that is said in the New Testament that implies a primacy in the apostolic college vested in Peter, and in this view we can but be struck with the evident exaggeration which pervades the whole argument of Wilberforce in his statements of the relation of Peter to the Church. In fact, the argument is overdone; for there is ascribed to Peter a peculiarity of office far beyond any thing hinted at in the Scriptures, and which nothing short of special revelation could warrant us in believing had devolved upon any successor.

The admission of a Primacy held by Peter in the original apostolic college, by no means involves an assent to the inference that the Bishop of Rome inherits that prerogative as his successor.

1. Peter held the primacy as an apostle, and it could be only an apostle in the full sense of the word that could in any way succeed to that office. The whole of Wilberforce's argument rests upon the assumption that the Apostolate is perpetuated in the Episcopate. This is the fallacy which underlies this whole discussion, on the Protestant as well as the Roman side. But it is directly contrary to Scripture. There is no evidence there that the apostles intended to convey their own peculiar functions to any of the ministers whom they appointed. The apostles were appointed by the Lord, with the words, "As my Father hath sent me so send I you." No such words passed upon any of the bishops whom the apostles ordained. They were not, as the Twelve were, "named apostles" (Luke vi. 13), and consequently could not enter upon their office. An apostle is "not of men, neither by man, but of Jesus Christ and God the Father" (Gal. i. 1)—directly called of God. It belonged not to the apostles to send other apostles, consequently any office or official rank which Peter held among his brethren derived from his apostolical character, he could not communicate; and if he could not impart the office of apostleship, much less could he that of apostolic Primacy.

2. It is an assumption that Peter ever really held the office of Bishop of the Church of Rome. I do not mean to call in question the ancient tradition that he and St. Paul were together at Rome, and united in founding the Church there; but if there, Peter was there as an

Apostle, establishing the Church, guarding it and setting it in order; and it was in so doing that he ordained Linus, as the tradition runs (though some authorities, I believe, refer the ordination of Linus to Paul, and that of Clement to Peter), as the bishop thereof during his lifetime, and not as his successor.

3. It is very clear that no such dignity was claimed by the earlier bishops of Rome after the apostolic age, as that of Primate over the whole Church. No trace of any assertion of any special dignity for that Church is apparent until some time in the second century. Now, it is absolutely incredible that it should have been so if the case really had been such as the defenders of the Papacy allege. Peter, when he wrote his Epistles, called himself the "Apostle of the Lord Jesus Christ." It was incumbent on him to assert his calling—to make known the relation in which he stood to the Church and to the Lord. Could it have been less so with one who was really his successor? But in the Epistle of Clement we see no such assertion of office—nothing that could suggest that he as Bishop of Rome had any preëminence over his brethren. It is an epistle written in the name of the Church of Rome to that of Corinth. Its temper is that of paternal admonition, and it contains nothing which implies any such superiority as Primacy.

The earliest indications of any thing like an assertion of a claim of Primacy that these Roman Catholic writers adduce, are as late as the third century. Cyprian is the earliest writer whom Wilberforce cites as calling the

Episcopal See of Rome "the chair of Peter." He refers to many authors as saying that Peter founded the See of Rome, and that Linus succeeded him, but nothing at that early period that implies that the Bishop of Rome inherited the prerogatives of the apostle. A respect is claimed for the Church of Rome as of ancient apostolic foundation, even as early as the time of the Quartodeciman controversy; but we are struck with the utter absence of any thing out of which the claim of papal supremacy could have grown.* One citation which Wilberforce makes from

* All that can be deduced from the references in the writers of the earlier centuries to the See of Rome is, that that Church had a peculiar dignity and consideration, as being of apostolic foundation. It was the Church that gave importance to the bishop rather than the bishop to the Church. It was the *Seat of Peter*, as it began to be called, that imparted authority to the bishop who occupied it, rather than the *successor of Peter*, that gave weight to the see. Thus Ffulkes says:

"That the See of Rome was supposed to possess some inherent prerogatives" (this is rather a stronger expression than the facts warrant) "no student of ecclesiastical history will now deny; and the most hostile explanation that can be given of them is, that they attached to it as the seat of empire. This may or may not be the fair inference to be drawn from those well-known canons of the second and fourth General Councils, in which rank 'next after Rome' is given to the See of Constantinople; but it is certainly fair to call attention to what they suppress as well as express. Constantinople had, in fact, no other title to put forward but that of its imperial importance. Rome, on the other hand, in addition to any mere imperial privileges, had another that had infinitely more charms for Christendom, namely, the preëminence of its apostolic origin. As it was the only see in the West which could boast of that distinction, so it was the only see in all the world that had been founded, not by one apostle, but by two, and those the greatest of the apostles. This, incomparably more than the other, is the fact so glowingly dwelt upon by Irenæus, Cyprian, Tertullian, Athanasius, Augustine, and others who have testified to the prerogatives of the See of Rome; and if they have nowhere defined those prerogatives, it is quite certain that both fathers and councils continually acted as recognizing in them a good deal more than mere words" (pp. 22, 23).

All the citations this author gives from those fathers go to this extent and no more; that the Church of Rome was entitled to respect and reverence,

Tertullian seems rather like irony. Complaining of the relaxation of discipline he says: "I hear that an edict has been propounded, and that a peremptory one: the Pontifex Maximus, it seems, that is the Bishop of bishops, gives out, I remit the crimes of adultery and fornication to the penitent;" and he adds that Tertullian, who had at that time become a Montanist, asserts that the apostle had received no other than a personal commission, and denies that the Church had any authority to readmit men to communion after deadly sins. The application of the term Pontifex Maximus, the title of the Pagan emperors to the Bishop of Rome, seems to imply that there was a tendency to exaggeration of the authority of that see, which he intended thus, by the use of satire, to condemn. The fact of his having become a Montanist does not impair the value of his testimony as to a matter of fact.

There is, however, in Wilberforce, a disposition to exaggerate every little circumstance which can be made to have the remotest bearing upon the point. It is only by aggregating such circumstances that he makes what seems a cumulative argument in favor of his position; but his argument is an inverted cone, and has a poor basis on which to rest a faith which must receive an institution so momentous in its influence, as a divine ordi nance. In fact, it is very apparent that the recognition

and her judgment as having special weight on account of her apostolic origin; but they do not involve the idea that the Bishop of Rome inherited all the authority of Peter. That, this very writer admits, was the result of a later development.

of the Papacy is a result of natural reason, and not of faith—an intellectual conclusion rather than a spiritual act.

4. It is admitted by these very writers that the Primacy of Peter was a very different thing from the Papal supremacy as it now appears. The latter has been the growth of centuries. Its development has been owing to political quite as much as to ecclesiastical causes; but the one principle which has given it vitality, has been the idea of unity—the necessity of some power which should be an ultimate appeal in cases of difficulty and doubt.

Says Ffulkes:

"At first it seemed as though the supreme governorship of the Church had been entrusted to the converted emperors. Constantine assumed it immediately after his victory over Maxentius, as a trust committed to him.

"On tidings of the rupture between Alexander and Arius, he despatched a joint letter to them both, in which one is censured for having raised imprudent questions, and the other for having returned rash answers. Unable to bring them to terms by his remonstrances, it was he who conceived and carried out the plan of calling all the bishops of Christendom together, to pronounce upon their case. Here is a fact of prime importance in ecclesiastical history. It should be written down in the largest characters, that what are called œcumenical councils, originated, not with the apostles or their successors, but with the first Christian emperor and his successors; so much so that there is not one of them, at least of those designated œcumenical by East and West, that was not convened by imperial mandate."

"Another notable feature of the Constitution of these councils was that they directly involved the notion of universal monarchy. * * *

"Gradually then as the whole Church assembled in œcumenical synod, it not only felt conscious of having been convened by one Sovereign potentate, but it likewise saw the bishop of one see sitting at the head of the collective episcopate. Could it have been otherwise than a mere question of time, to delegate to him the same executive powers over Christendom generally, that had been already delegated to metropolitans over provincial, and to patriarchs over diocesan Churches? Could it have been otherwise regarded than as carrying out of received principles to their legitimate results; a logical consequence of assimilating ecclesiastical jurisdiction to that of the empire—the universal Church to the universal State?"

Again:

"In the matter of appeals likewise, there can be no doubt but that Constantine and his successors received them from all parts of Christendom, and appointed judges to hear them, whose sentence they confirmed and executed. Previously, there had been no one Supreme Court of appeal in the Church; now, there was not only one, but it vested in one supreme potentate. There is not a heresy, from that of Paul of Samosata, nor a schism from that of Donatus, of any consequence for the first six centuries, in which their intervention is not recorded in some form or other. The earliest ecclesiastical historian had styled Constantine a "common bishop;" the next in order, far from disputing it, expresses himself as follows in a studied preface: We include the emperors in our history, because from the time that they became Christian, ecclesiastical affairs have depended on them, and the greatest councils have been and are held by their decree."—*Ffulkes*, pp. 17–20.

This view of the case is an admission that the recognition at last of the supremacy of the Pope of Rome, did not spring from any faith in it as a divine institution, but was in effect a conventional arrangement, which grew out of the experienced necessity of some central authority for the purpose of maintaining unity. The most that can be claimed for it is, that it was providentially ordered and allowed.

It requires nothing more than the admissions and arguments of these writers to establish the conclusion that the government of the Church under the Papacy is an essentially different constitution from that administered by the apostles in the first age of the Church.

The Papacy is an ecclesiastical monarchy, which

claims to be universal—coextensive with Christendom. The Church was constituted a universal spiritual polity, not yet arrived at the condition of a kingdom, but the kingdom in a mystery to be revealed in its perfection, at the return of the King from heaven.

The rule of the Church in the hands of the first Apostles, was authority administered by a commission in constant communication through associated Prophets with the Head in the heavens, receiving thus intimations of His mind, and endowed with wisdom to carry the same into effect.

Under the Papacy the Church is governed by a Viceroy, for whose administration infallibility is claimed, but without any associated ordinances for ascertaining the mind of the Lord. The Papacy is an anticipation of the Kingdom, and a usurpation of the place of the Lord Himself. The term *vicar of Christ* implies that a single man can adequately fill the place of the Lord. A collective headship, consisting of a number called by the Lord to be His representatives, is free from this objection, while, at the same time, it satisfies the idea of a Catholic Supremacy. No substitute can perfectly fill the place of the Lord Himself. At His second coming He appears as sole Head. In His absence He is represented, not by one, but by Twelve, acting as one.

One of the strongest arguments for the Papacy has been the assumption that it is the only way of solving the problem of unity. If, then, any other way can be shown as possible, this argument is so far neutralized.

If an alternative can be presented, it proves nothing indeed, but it relieves the mind from what might otherwise be regarded as a logical necessity. An hypothesis or a possibility is not, indeed, an argument, but to certain states of mind it has at least the effect of a negative argument. And so if it is shown that there is any other way by which Catholic unity can be realized than by the admission of the divine authority of the Papacy, such a suggestion tends to weaken in so far the force of arguments which might otherwise seem to some minds irresistible in its support.

Such an hypothesis I have presented as a means of solving this problem. I hope it may at least serve the purpose of relieving some minds of embarrassing difficulties.

CHAPTER VII.

THE CONSTITUENT UNITIES.

Principles announced by St. Paul—One Body—One Spirit—One Hope—One Lord—One Faith—One Baptism—One God and Father of All—These the Principles by which Unity was to be preserved, and by which it is to be recovered—Theological aspect of these principles—Necessity of going back to first principles.

In the preceding pages the unity of the Spirit has been considered as a result. The words of St. Paul that have been already referred to, in the fourth chapter of the Epistle to the Ephesians, present to us several *constituent unities*, all of which must be apprehended in order to the realization of the all-comprehensive unity. To these, in conclusion, I propose briefly to call attention.

"There is one Body and one Spirit, even as ye are called in one Hope of your calling, one Lord, one Faith, one Baptism, one God and Father of all, who is above all, and through all, and in you all." Let us consider them in detail.

1. *One Body.*—Not many bodies united in a confederation, but one universal body. This is directly at variance with the notion of a variety of sects or sectarian organizations, and implies plainly that there can be no

unity of the Spirit where separate ecclesiastical organization is maintained and justified. It may not be clear how the existing evil is to be at once overcome—it may be unavoidable for a time that the existence of sects should be allowed; but there can be no approximation to unity on the part of any individuals or communities by whom the sectarian condition is not disapproved and deprecated, and regarded only as an evil from which in time the Church is to be delivered. Consequently, no movements toward a confederation in which the respective interests of the confederated sects are to be preserved, can be regarded as any approach to unity. The body is one, and its unity must be made manifest in every part and member, just as in the natural body the life is whole in every part.

This conviction of the essential oneness of the body would have the effect to suppress active measures of sectarian proselyting, and rather turn the attention of men to the inquiry how they and their brethren could be delivered from the evils of division, and enabled to attain the unity of the Spirit. This would remove one of the greatest evils of sectarianism, and incline Christian men to recognize the good that is in their brethren as well as to see and object to the evil. There can be no return to God without repentance, and the first fruits of repentance will be to renounce and condemn the sectarian principle in whatever form it may present itself.

2. *One Spirit.*—The sectarian principle divides the Spirit. Instead of looking for diverse forms of mani-

festation in one body, it requires a distinct form of manifestation in each different body. This is its alleged justification. The plea is made that all men are not alike, and that the manifestation of the Spirit must be different in different classes as well as individuals; and in order thereto, these classes, with their different intellectual, æsthetic, and social tendencies, must be separately organized. What is the consequence? First of all, the manifestation of the Spirit is hindered, because a partial operation can never be complete; and then each separate portion is hindered by its separation from sharing in the grace which may come to the others. This theory by which sects are justified is not warranted by facts. Whatever grace through the forbearance and long-suffering of God may be found in one sect or section does not avail for others. The spirit of antagonism, or of sectarian or denominational self-interest, hinders each sect from deriving benefit from the good that is in the others. The good that is in the Roman Catholic Church has little power over the Protestant, and *vice versâ*. The peculiar features of spiritual grace that appear in the Episcopalian bodies, operate with very limited effect upon non-Episcopalians; and so on throughout the catalogue. True it is that the Protestant Reformation had a powerful influence upon the Roman Catholic Church, in compelling a "reformation in the head and members," which had for centuries been called for within the Church to no purpose. Methodism had a powerful effect in arousing the Church of England from its apathy and indifference to the spiritual wants of the masses in England. Every onward movement, every true revival of a part, has had an effect upon other parts; more, however, in the way of provoking to emulation than in the more excellent way of a general diffusion of life through the whole body. But it still remains, that when the Spirit of God acts at all in a divided Church, His action is divided, and all parts do not feel alike the movement of the pulses of the divine life. For the full manifestation of the power of the One Spirit there must be one body, in which all the members are organically knit together, holding the Head and drawing nourishment from Him by the joints and bands by which they are united, so that it may increase with the increase of God (Coloss. ii. 19).

3. *One Hope.*—The hope which St. Paul referred to was the hope of the Lord's second Coming, and of our gathering together unto Him (1 Thess. i. 10; 2 Thess. ii. 1). This was the "one hope of their calling," which, giving to all of them a common object of interest, tended powerfully to remove causes of division. This hope involved the perfecting of the body, and its being "presented as a chaste virgin to Christ" at His appearing (2 Cor. xi. 2). It was not the mere hope of happiness after death—of individual salvation—but a hope for the body, the Church—an interest in the Body as the instrument God would use for the fulfilment of His purposes toward creation (Ephes. iii. 10, 11)—that Paul here refers to. The influence of such a hope in drawing faithful men to-

gether, and in exciting them to endeavor to keep the unity of the Spirit, must be obvious. With such an end in view—the participation of the glory of the risen Lord, reigning with Him in His kingdom, and serving under Him in the government and rule of the universe—an end which can only be attained by the Church perfected in unity—an end which separation and disunion must frustrate and postpone—the motive to preserve unity would be most strong, as the sympathy and fellowship it would inspire would be deep and intimate.

The loss of this hope removes, therefore, one of the strongest influences which is to bind into one the members of the body of Christ. Its recovery is one of the essential conditions of any approach toward unity. There can be no progress in that direction without this as the common end and object of all desire.

It is to be observed that in the attempt to effect the union of sects, a common hope seems to have been overlooked as one of the essential constituents of unity. And truly, the mere hope of individual salvation, which is all that the popular religion dwells upon, has little in it to bind men into one, since no sect—not even the Roman Catholic practically—really affirms that salvation is not possible out of its communion.

If, however, we rise up to the higher ground of a hope for the Church—for the body of Christ, as the Perfect Bride of the Lamb to be prepared for the marriage—to be caught away, and come with Him when He shall appear in His glory, a different object is presented to view. Individual salvation is lost sight of, and all personal interests are swallowed up in the one Hope of the glory which shall be conferred upon the Bride of the Lamb. Here is a motive to unity, and a force operative to effect it.

4. *One Lord.*—Jesus Christ is the Lord. God hath given Him power over all flesh. All power is given unto Him in heaven and on earth. All things are to be brought into subjection unto Him. He is to be revealed as King of kings, and Lord of lords. He is Lord, not as in right of His Godhead, but as the prerogative of His manhood, for Lordship was the Father's gift to Him in reward of His obedience as man. We see not yet all things put under Him. In this present dispensation the Church is the sphere where His Lordship is exercised and acknowledged, and this acknowledgment is one of the essentials of unity. There must be conceded to Him the right to do His pleasure in His own house. Neither directly nor by implication must men deprive Him of that right, claiming to shape the constitution of the Church according to their own conceits, or denying Him the right to call from the Heavens and send forth those whom He may choose, to rule and order His house according to the will of His Father.

He must be seen as One Lord. But how can the one lordship be seen in the Church when there is no recognized centre from which the Head can communicate with all the parts, and direct their movements toward a common end; but every fragment has its own self-imposed constitution, and struggles to get itself a place and name of honor at the expense of its rivals?

Jesus Christ was sent to be both a Prince and a Saviour. His Lordship therefore—His right to rule, requires distinct recognition. In words, the Lordship of Christ would not be denied by any who profess to believe the Gospel; but closer thought upon the subject, would disclose a significance in these words which would be found to reveal some of the causes of existing divisions, and to suggest their remedy.

5. *One Faith.*—By this is meant, doubtless, the Faith once delivered to the Saints: the great facts of the Gospel history, with the truths which they involve as affirmed in the Apostles', and afterwards expanded in the Nicene creed. The Incarnation, sufferings, resurrection, and ascension of our Lord Jesus Christ; His coming again to judge the living and the dead; the sending of the Holy Ghost; the calling of the Church; the resurrection of the body and the life everlasting, as the same is revealed in the Scriptures. This is the one Faith, and it is implied that it must be held as one—with a common conviction—a common interpretation. The same formula held, with variant interpretations, would not be an element of unity, but the reverse. As this point has come under our consideration in previous chapters, I need not dwell upon it here.

6. *One Baptism.*—Into the One Name, of the Father, the Son, and the Holy Ghost; for one end—the remission of sins; knitting the baptized mysteriously into one

body, of which they are thus constituted members. This is one of the elements of unity and must be recognized as such—the outward ordinance, the means of initiation—implying that the body is a real, visible constitution; as necessary as the faith of which it is the Seal. And this involves, also, an apprehension of the standing into which the Baptized are brought as the members of Christ and partakers of His grace.

7. *One God and Father of all, who is above all, and through all, and in you all.*

These words serve to complete the circle of unities in which the unity of the Spirit has its full exercise. We are not to understand that St. Paul here designed to assert the unity of the Godhead as against the Pagan mythology. Nor will this text serve any purpose of sustaining Unitarian doctrine. The Father is the one source of all being; every thing that exists proceeds from Him as the one fountain of existence, and no enumeration of the great principles of truth by which the unity of the Spirit is effected would be complete without leading up to Him from whom all things proceed. The "One Spirit" has been named, who dwells and manifests His presence in One Body; the "One Lord Jesus Christ" who is the Son of God, of the same substance with the Father; and now we are led up to the "One God and Father of all, who is above all, and through all, and in you all." These last words, "in you all," may, perhaps, be regarded as the specially significant words in this passage. The oneness of the members of Christ in the Father and the Son, is, as was shown in the first chapter, the ultimate reality, and in order to the preservation of the unity of the Spirit, this truth must be seen and apprehended.

Since, then, these are the principles by the apprehension of which the unity of the Spirit which existed at the first was to be preserved, it is by the same principles that unity now broken, must be recovered. Their consideration covers a wide field—nothing less, in fact, than the whole field of Theology as related to the Church. This is a branch of theology that has been much overlooked, and, in fact, among non-Episcopalian Protestants, almost universally ignored. The subject of the Church has been treated as a side issue, of secondary importance, or none at all. It has not, in the received theological systems of the day, been regarded as having any relation to the inward life, and the assertion of any principles in regard to it is almost always denounced as bigotry.

The ancient creeds included the Church—the Holy Catholic Church, as an article of the Faith. It stands with the Incarnation—the mission of the Holy Ghost—the life everlasting. This would seem to suggest that the doctrine concerning the Church was equal in importance to the others with which it is associated in the most ancient symbols, and had some intimate connection with them. And what does it involve? Plainly the relations which the Lord Jesus Christ sustains to the body which the Father has chosen out of the world—the manner and form in which He exercises His rule upon the earth—the means and ordinances by which He dispenses His grace—the way in which the Father is to be worshipped, and the purpose to be accomplished by the Church. All these are questions essentially theological, as much so as the doctrines of Incarnation and atonement, and involve principles upon which Christian people should not be left in doubt or uncertainty.

But these are questions which are for the most part ignored or put out of sight. It is contended that they are not *essential.* If by this is meant that a full recognition of them is not an absolute *sine qua non* of individual salvation, it may be admitted. But as the purpose of God involves something more than the salvation of individuals, even the perfecting of the Bride of His Son, the truth is not to be regarded exclusively in its relation to the salvation of individuals. Whatever is requisite to the completeness of the system of divine revelation is *essential*, however it may or may not affect individual salvation. "Every word of God is pure," and no individual, much more no Church, is perfect and complete in all the will of God, which does not hold to and assert all that God has revealed regarding the relations of the Church, as well as of individuals to the Lord.

It is only when these which I have called *constituent unities* are apprehended, that the true nature and necessity of unity can be seen at all. Without them the different religious communities are only so many voluntary societies, with no common bond ; and although they may agree to differ, they never can attain to that higher and mysterious unity which is a reflex of that in the Most Holy.

It would seem, therefore, that it is necessary to go back to first principles in order to any progress toward the true unity of the Spirit. The recovery of unity is not a matter of feeling, but of principle. Any coming together of divided sects upon the mere ground of good feeling, of kindness of heart, of mutual personal confidence, would not fulfil the conditions of unity. Something is gained when Christian bodies that have been separated or have grown asunder, have ceased to bite and devour one another, and have come to recognize the good that is in those from whom they are separated. This may be regarded as a step in advance, an improvement upon that time when every sect regarded it as its chief duty to oppose and contend with all who did not subscribe to all its usages and dogmas. Still more is gained when different sects or parties are so enabled to enlarge their basis of doctrine as to merge their differences without compromising their convictions. But the real value of any movements of this nature is in their tendency to lead Christian men to see more clearly the constituent unities—the apostolically announced principles which are requisite to preserving the unity of the Spirit in the bond of peace. Existing prejudices and long-standing convictions are hindrances to the recognition of a system that is materially different from what has been received, however logically it may be presented; and it is, therefore, necessary to go back to first principles in order to change the position from which the subject is seen, and enable the observer to view it in new lights and relations.

In presenting the views set forth in the previous pages, the writer has not overlooked this difficulty, or been unaware of the hindrances which the reception of the popular religious system presents to the admission of the conclusions here exhibited. But a sharp contrast is sometimes more effectual to awaken thought than an easy transition. The movements that succeed in changing the face of society are those which are radical, and such is the character of the doctrine defended in these pages. The unity here proposed is radically different from that popularly assumed, even in the Episcopalian bodies, and as such it claims the attention of thoughtful Christian men. There is no point of contact between a system which involves a truly Catholic organization, and one which looks no further than the confederation of a number of voluntary societies. Dread of the Papacy has, doubtless, precluded, on the part of Protestants, all thoughts of Catholicity; but if that evil can be avoided, the subject may be more candidly considered. And then, if the minds of Christian men can be raised up to the recognition of a constant supernatural presence of the Holy Ghost in the Church, they may be enabled to see, first, the possibility, and afterwards the reality of a divine interposition to restore the long lost unity of the Body of Christ.

But the writer would not urge upon any, hasty or inconsiderate changes in their Church relations. The movements of isolated individuals, however they may affect themselves, have little or no effect upon the general result of the recovery of unity. It is in the performance of duty in the relations in which one is providentially placed, that light upon one's path is received, and the will of God made known. Activity of mind, interest in questions of importance, is of more consequence than the right or wrong determinations of individuals. When there is activity, the truth has some chance; when the general mind is dull and sluggish, truth and error alike pass unheded.

The first condition of any progress in a right direction will be a conviction that there is a radical error in the generally received views of this subject. This will open a place for repentance, and without repentance there can be no return. Departure from the ways of God, however insensibly it may have been fallen into, can only be healed by repentance. What shall be the substitute for the received system must be learned from the study of Holy Scripture, and for this I have endeavored to furnish some help. The existing condition of the religious world, one would think, was enough to prove that an error nothing less than radical held possession of the consciences of men, and that a great and radical change was required.

And this change is not one that can be postponed for centuries. The signs of the times warn us that the period of fierce and active conflict with the powers of

Antichrist is near at hand, when all the strength that can be drawn from a divinely ordained unity will be needed to defend each and every individual from the seductive power which shall come with "all deceiveableness of unrighteousness." It is only as members of the Body of His Son that we receive the grace of God; and it is only in the faith of that membership that we can "withstand in the evil day." That faith may be firm, we must stand in unity, and not in separateness. Sectarianism takes away the defences, and leaves those who are infected by it open to all the assaults of the adversary. Blindly, unconsciously, are men and communities now being led into error and unbelief, because they recognize no divine ordinances whereby they may be bound together in the support and confession of the Faith.

When Babylon, the city of confusion, is destroyed, then shall those in whom the unity of the Father and the Son is manifested, appear united as the chaste and unspotted Bride of the Lamb, ready for the marriage.

www.ingramcontent.com/pod-product-compliance
Lightning Source LLC
LaVergne TN
LVHW021425110826
845150LV00007B/2083
9781425508494